APR 8 - 2004

The
Caribbean

Anne Wallace Sharp

LUCENT BOOKS®

THOMSON

GALE

San Diego • Detroit • New York • San Francisco • Cleveland • New Haven, Conn. • Waterville, Maine • London • Munich

© 2003 by Lucent Books. Lucent Books is an imprint of The Gale Group, Inc.,
a division of Thomson Learning, Inc.

Lucent Books™ and Thomson Learning ™ are trademarks used herein under license.

For more information, contact
Lucent Books
27500 Drake Rd.
Farmington Hills, MI 48331-3535
Or you can visit our Internet site at http://www.gale.com

LIBRARY OF CONGRESS CATALOGING-IN-PUBLICATION DATA

Sharp, Anne Wallace.
   The Caribbean / by Anne Wallace Sharp
      v. cm. — (Indigenous peoples of the world)
Includes bibliographical references and index.
Summary: Discusses the history, geography, and culture of the indigenous peoples of the
Caribbean. Topics include: everyday life, society, beliefs, colonialism, Amerindians today,
and the future.
   ISBN 1-59018-271-5 (hardback : alk. paper)
  1. Indians of the West Indies—Juvenile literature. [1. Indians of the West Indies.]
I. Title. II. Indigenous peoples of the world (San Diego, Calif.).
   F1619.S53 2003
   972.9004'97—dc21

                                    2003001642

Printed in the U.S.A.

Contents

Foreword

Nearly every area of the world has indigenous populations, those people who are descended from the original settlers of a given region, often arriving many millennia ago. Many of these populations exist today despite overwhelming odds against their continuing survival.

Though indigenous populations have come under attack for a variety of reasons, in most cases land lies at the heart of the conflict. The hunger for land has threatened indigenous societies throughout history, whether the aggressor was a neighboring tribe or a foreign culture. The reason for this is simple: For indigenous populations, *way of life* has nearly always depended on the land and its bounty. Indeed, cultures from the Inuit of the frigid Arctic to the Yanomami of the torrid Amazon rain forest have been indelibly shaped by the climate and geography of the regions they inhabit.

As newcomers moved into already settled areas of the world, competition led to tension and violence. When newcomers possessed some important advantage—greater numbers or more powerful weapons—the results were predictable. History is rife with examples of outsiders triumphing over indigenous populations. Anglo-Saxons and Vikings, for instance, moved into eastern Europe and the British Isles at the expense of the indigenous Celts. Europeans traveled south through Africa and into Australia displacing the indigenous Bushmen and Aborigines, while other Westerners ventured into the Pacific at the expense of the indigenous Melanesians, Micronesians, and Polynesians. And in North and South America, the colonization of the New World by European powers resulted in the decimation and displacement of numerous Native American groups.

Nevertheless, many indigenous populations retained their identity and managed to survive. Only in the last one hundred years, however, have anthropologists begun to study with any objectivity the hundreds of indigenous societies found throughout the world. And only within the last few decades have these societies been truly appreciated and acknowledged for their richness and complexity. The ability to adapt to and manage their environments is but one marker of the incredible resourcefulness of many indigenous populations. The Inuit, for example, created two distinct modes of travel for getting around the barren, icy region that is their home. The sleek, speedy kayak —with its whalebone frame and sealskin cover—allowed the Inuit to silently skim the waters of the nearby ocean and bays.

And the sledge (or dogsled)—with its caribou-hide platform and runners built from whalebone or frozen fish covered with sealskin—made travel over the snow- and ice-covered landscape possible.

The Indigenous Peoples of the World series strives to present a clear and realistic picture of the world's many and varied native cultures. The series captures the uniqueness as well as the similarities of indigenous societies by examining family and community life, traditional spirituality and religion, warfare, adaptation to the environment, and interaction with other native and nonnative peoples.

The series also offers perspective on the effects of Western civilization on indigenous populations as well as a multifaceted view of contemporary life. Many indigenous societies, for instance, struggle today with poverty, unemployment, racism, poor health, and a lack of educational opportunities. Others find themselves embroiled in political instability, civil unrest, and violence. Despite the problems facing these societies, many indigenous populations have regained a sense of pride in themselves and their heritage. Many also have experienced a resurgence of traditional art and culture as they seek to find a place for themselves in the modern world.

The Indigenous Peoples of the World series offers an in-depth study of different regions of the world and the people who have long inhabited those regions. All books in the series include fully documented primary and secondary source quotations that enliven the text. Sidebars highlight notable events, personalities, and traditions, while annotated bibliographies offer ideas for future research. Numerous maps and photographs provide the reader with a pictorial glimpse of each society.

From the Aborigines of Australia to the various indigenous peoples of the Caribbean, Europe, South America, Mexico, Asia, and Africa, the series covers a multitude of societies and their cultures. Each book stands alone and the series as a collection offers valuable comparisons of the past history and future problems of the indigenous peoples of the world.

Who Are the Indigenous People of the Caribbean?

During the last Ice Age, some fifteen to twenty thousand years ago, prehistoric men from Asia, while hunting giant mammoths and other animals, crossed the frozen Bering Strait with their families and entered the continent of North America. From present-day Alaska, these people, the original Amerindians, continued to migrate over North America and gradually made their way southward into Mexico and South America. These descendants of the original hunters formed new tribes and new ways of life wherever they settled. From the tip of North America and the interior of South America, several groups of Amerindians would eventually find their way to the islands of the Caribbean.

The Caribbean and Its Original Inhabitants

The Caribbean, a chain of islands that lies in a long sweeping curve at the western end of the Atlantic Ocean between South and North America, beckoned the Indians with an abundance of natural riches. The tropi-cal climate of the region, with an average daily temperature in the high seventies, offered opportunities for bountiful harvests and unlimited fishing. The isolation of the islands also provided a safe haven from former enemies and a place to nurture their growing populations.

Four distinct groups of Amerindians once occupied the various islands of the Caribbean—the Ciboney, Lucayan, Arawak or Taino, and the Carib. Together their total numbers are estimated to have exceeded 4 million by 1492 when Christopher Columbus arrived in the area.

The Ciboney and Lucayan

The Ciboney, who once lived in the western parts of the islands known today as Cuba and Hispaniola (Haiti and the Dominican Republic), migrated from the North American continent nearly five thousand years ago. Also known as the Siboney, these people lived a simple life in small groups near the banks of rivers and streams and all along the island coastlines. They lived off the land; hunted small animals, reptiles, and birds; and gathered wild plants. They did not plant crops but did make tools out of stone, bone, or wood. As the Ciboney drifted south and east, they were turned back by other Amerindians and absorbed into other tribes. They had ceased to exist as a people long before the Europeans set foot in the Caribbean.

The Lucayans also lived a simple life and subsisted mainly on fish caught with bone fishhooks. They also grew cotton and supplemented their diet with corn and other vegetables. The Lucayans lived on the various islands of the Bahamas and have the distinction of being the first Amerindians to encounter Christopher Columbus and his men. Within twenty years of Columbus's arrival, however, the Lucayans were extinct. Other than a few brief men-

tions in the explorer's journal, historians have little solid information about this tribe of native Americans or Amerindians, a term generally preferred by historians.

The Arawak or Taino

The Arawak or Taino, who made their homes on the islands of Puerto Rico and Hispaniola, were undoubtedly the most populous group of Caribbean Amerindians. The first Arawaks to enter the Caribbean were a group of hunters and gatherers from the Orinoco and Amazon river basins of South America. They settled in communities, built waterproof houses, and made high-quality pottery that is on display in selected museums around the world. Around A.D. 500 a more advanced group of Arawak began to explore and settle other islands and also move into the interiors of the bigger

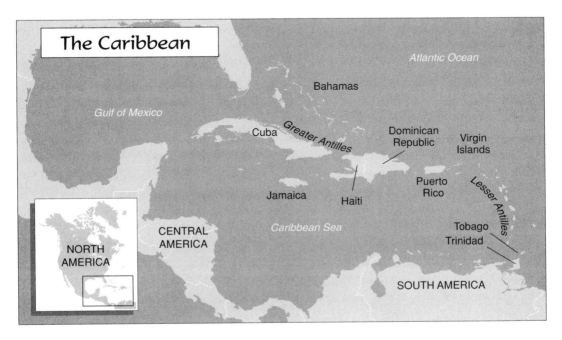

islands. This group was made up of skilled craftsworkers who used well-made tools and produced beautiful stonework.

A third group of Arawak appeared on the scene around A.D. 1000 and came to be known as the Taino. Highly skilled in shell and gold work, the Taino were even more advanced, both culturally and architecturally, than early Arawaks. According to a group of scholars who maintain a Taino website, "The Taino culture was the most developed in the Caribbean when Columbus reached Hispaniola in 1492."[1] At one time the Taino inhabited an area that stretched from present-day Florida south through the islands of the Caribbean into the coastal area of South America, as far as Brazil.

Amerindians greet Christopher Columbus in 1492. The Taino were the most populous Amerindians in the Caribbean when Columbus arrived.

The Carib

The Taino lived peacefully and prosperously in the Caribbean until the early thirteenth century when a group of fierce and warlike Indians known as the Carib began moving northward from South America into the Caribbean. The Carib originated in the valley of the Amazon River in South America and ultimately occupied various regions of South and Central America and parts of the Caribbean. In fact, the Caribbean Sea and the entire region are named after them. They began their northward migration around A.D. 1200 and within one hundred years were expanding into all areas of the Caribbean.

Trinidad was the first island in the Caribbean that was occupied by the Carib. This island eventually became the center of a vast Carib network of trade and exchange. From Trinidad, the Carib also began raiding various other islands where they captured, killed, or expelled the Taino. In her book *Islands* writer Louise B. Young reports that the Carib accomplished their goal by "arriving secretly by night, carrying off men, women, and children in canoes."[2]

The Spanish believed the ferocious Carib were cannibals and called them *canibales,* from which the word *cannibal* originated. Historians theorize that if the Europeans had not come to the New World, the Carib, who had reached the Virgin Islands by 1492, would probably have exterminated the Arawak and continued their expansion throughout the Caribbean. As it happened, the Carib expansion was stalled on the island of Puerto Rico by the sheer number of Taino living there and by a common enemy: the Spanish.

The Caribbean Today

Unlike the Lucayans and Ciboney, the Taino and the Carib survived the arrival and subsequent attacks of the Europeans. While virtually absent from the historical record for hundreds of years and even believed extinct, the Taino and Carib are today enjoying a resurgence of their heritage and culture.

The total population of the Caribbean today is about 36 million. Of this figure only a small portion are Amerindian. Nonetheless, the Taino of Puerto Rico are alive and well, as are the Carib Indians who live on the islands of Trinidad, Saint Vincent, and Dominica.

The Caribbean Islands today are among the most ethnically diverse in the world with their colorful mix of cultures, people, and lifestyles. Evidence of the region's long and dynamic history, including its Amerindian influence, can be found in all areas of modern life.

This photo offers an aerial view of a bay in Saint Thomas, Virgin Islands, where Caribbean Indians still make their home.

Chapter 1

Adapting to Life in the Caribbean

The first written description of the Caribbean islands comes from explorer Christopher Columbus, who in late 1492 made the following notation in his journal: "Islands with lofty mountains . . . most beautiful and of a thousand shapes . . . filled with trees of many kinds and tall, and they seem to touch the sky."[3]

Each island in the Caribbean is unique. Many offer sandy beaches and luscious palm trees and other greenery, while others feature breathtaking volcanic backdrops and thick rain forests. All, however, feature warm climates, adequate rainfall, and an abundance of natural riches.

These gifts of nature seemed to offer the Amerindians everything they wanted in order to live prosperous and comfortable lives. With bountiful harvests and abundant fish, the Taino and Carib Indians were able to form stable island populations who lived entirely off the land and thrived in virtual isolation for hundreds of years.

In order to reach the islands of the Caribbean, both the Taino and the Carib re- lied on large dugout canoes. Both groups, in fact, were accomplished canoe makers, as well as expert users of these vessels.

Canoe Making

To make a dugout canoe, Amerindian men chopped down large trees such as the ceiba using stone or wooden axes and other tools. The enormous tree trunks were then hollowed out with smaller hand tools and also by the use of fire. Once the tree trunk had been burned, the remaining wood was easier to work with than raw green timber. Cross- pieces were then forced into position in order to widen the beam of the canoe. Once com- pleted, the canoes were capable of crossing the open sea while holding up to 150 people.

The Taino used their canoes primarily for fishing and for traveling from one island to another for the purpose of trade. In addi- tion to traveling throughout the different islands, the Taino also made frequent trips to the mainland of South America and parts of Central America. There they conducted trade and generally carried out peaceful missions with the indigenous people of those regions. Historian Alvin M. Josephy Jr. elaborates: "In time, a canoe-borne commerce and peaceful cultural contacts had burgeoned between the Arawakian islands and Mesoamerica."[4]

In addition to trade, the Carib also used their canoes for war, assembling fleets that sometimes included up to one hundred sail-fitted dugout canoes. The sails were made out of palm leaves. Historians agree that the Carib were hardy and daring sailors who paddled and sailed fearlessly from island to island.

Choosing a Village Site

Once the Amerindians landed on an island, their most important task was to choose and secure a good location for a village. Several factors were important in making this decision. For the Carib, who almost always chose to live near the sea, a site was selected on a good sand beach where the people could easily pull up their canoes. An offshore reef was essential to provide enough fish to feed the village.

The Carib preferred to live near the sea not only because their diet consisted mainly of fish, but because a coastal location facilitated communication with the Carib on other islands and enabled them to see approaching enemies in the event of war. For purposes of defense, the Carib usually settled on the windward side (the side that faced the direction from which the wind was blowing) of an island. This side

Amerindians burn out the inside of a tree trunk to make a dugout canoe. The Taino and Carib used their canoes to travel from island to island.

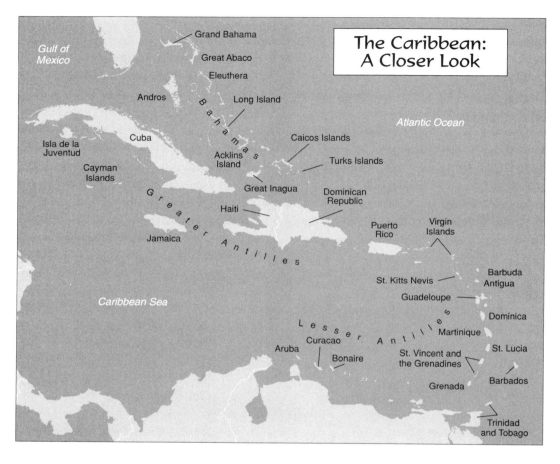

The Caribbean:
A Closer Look

generally had the roughest water and the highest cliffs, making the site harder to attack.

For those Amerindians settling in the interior, the most important factor in choosing a location was a source of fresh water. Many of the smaller islands had no large rivers and thus did not have enough drinking water to support a permanent settlement. Most of the Taino chose to settle on the larger, wetter, and better-forested islands.

Taino villages were built close to these sources of water. A tall fence usually sur-rounded the entire village, while a road was often built leading directly to the water source. Because water was scarce, guards were often posted nearby to protect the area from any possible invaders.

A Taino village, or *yucayeque,* was usu-ally built around a central plaza where the chief's house stood. The plaza was used for village meetings, celebrations, and other im-portant events. Other open areas were used for the ball games the Taino played. Villages and towns were of all sizes but sometimes quite large, containing several hundred dwellings. Around the village, outside the fence, were the farms and fields.

Finding Shelter

Shelter has always been essential in the Caribbean. The hot tropical sun can be relentless and problematic especially in the summer, but even more dangerous are the rains and wind that frequently buffet the islands. The Amerindians compensated for the local weather by constructing homes that provided the occupants both a comfortable and a safe shelter, using only the materials available on the islands.

The Taino used two primary architectural styles for their homes. The chiefs had spacious rectangular dwellings, called *bohios,* that often featured small porches. The ordinary people also had spacious houses but they were round with conical roofs made of branches and vines, tightly interwoven on a frame of small poles and covered with heavy palm leaves. Called *caneyes,* these structures had earthen floors, no windows, and little furniture.

Both *bohios* and *caneyes* could easily hold a family group of five to ten men and their entire extended family. It was not

The Islands of the Caribbean

Three distinct groups of islands make up the area of the world known as the Caribbean. These groups are the Bahamas, the Greater Antilles, and the Lesser Antilles. The word "Antilles" comes from the Latin word *ante,* meaning "before." It was Christopher Columbus who applied this name to the various groups of islands. He believed the islands were located "just before" the continent of Asia.

Strictly speaking, the Bahamas are not a geographic part of the Caribbean; the more than seven hundred islands that comprise this group actually lie in the Atlantic Ocean and not the Caribbean Sea. However, the Bahamas have historically and politically been included in all studies of the Caribbean.

The largest islands of the Caribbean belong to those included in the Greater Antilles. This grouping includes Cuba, Jamaica, Puerto Rico, and the two countries that comprise the island of Hispaniola—the Dominican Republic and Haiti. South and east of Puerto Rico is the group of islands known as the Lesser Antilles. This group contains Trinidad, Tobago, Dominica, Barbados, Aruba, and hundreds of other islands.

The Greater and Lesser Antilles were formed by volcanic action from a massive mountain range, most of which still lies under the sea. These islands have very complex environments and extremely fertile soil. This fertility has produced lush greenery and bountiful rainforests.

Tropical Hurricanes and Volcanoes

The Caribbean is noted for the number of hurricanes that strike there every year. The word hurricane, in fact, comes from the Arawak word *huracán,* their god of evil winds. Hurricane season usually runs from June to November, with an average of six storms striking the islands each year.

Hurricanes develop over the ocean, usually in the eastern Caribbean during the summer months when the sea surface temperature is high and the air pressure falls. These conditions create an "eye" around which a steep pressure gradient forms that is capable of generating wind at speeds of seventy-five miles an hour or more.

In November 1994 tropical storm Gordon swept across Haiti, causing massive flooding and over eight hundred deaths.

More than ten thousand people were left homeless on the island. Hurricane winds can sometimes reach in excess of two hundred miles per hour as they did when Hurricane Gilbert struck the island of Jamaica.

Volcanic eruptions are also common in the Caribbean as a result of the volcanic origin of many of the islands. In 1902 Mount Pelée on the island of Martinique in the Lesser Antilles erupted, sending a cloud of burning ash over much of the island. The eruption killed the entire population of the town of Saint Pierre. Only one man survived—a prisoner awaiting trial in a cell with walls so thick that they were not destroyed. This eruption caused the greatest loss of life—about forty thousand dead—due to volcanic action in the twentieth century.

The thick wall of this prison cell kept the only survivor of the 1902 eruption of Mount Pelée safe.

unusual, in fact, for some Taino homes to house as many as one hundred people.

Carib houses were generally rectangular with one end kept separate from the house and used primarily to store household utensils, tools, and weapons. The homes of both the Taino and the Carib were open-sided and often built on stilts. Although built of what modern architects would call flimsy material, Amerindian homes, if properly sited and constructed, were capable of withstanding the strong winds and hurricanes of the Caribbean.

Home Furnishings

Taino and Carib people usually slept on hammocks, called *amais* in Carib society, or on simple mats made out of banana leaves. Babies generally slept in wooden cradles. At night the huts were lighted with candles that were made from a sweet-smelling gum.

The Carib generally sat on stools made from polished red and yellow wood. The Taino, on the other hand, were noted for their skilled artistry in carving and decorating special wooden chairs called *duhos*. The *duhos* had woven seats but the legs and back were often carved in human or animal shapes. Prestige and power were intimately linked to the ownership and use of the seats. The *duhos* of the chiefs and other nobility were like thrones and often embellished with gold, shell, and bone decorations. They were carved with either high or low backs, depending on the owner's degree of status. The Spanish later reported that the high-backed *duhos* were used exclusively by the chiefs and nobility.

Christopher Columbus later described one of these chairs in his journal. "These are the most peculiar chairs," he wrote. "Each was made in one piece and in a strange shape resembling a short-legged animal with a tail as broad as the seat. This tail lifted up to make a back to lean against."[5]

Clothing

Neither the Taino nor the Carib wore much in the way of clothing. Amerindian men usually wore nothing, while some married Taino women sometimes wore a short skirt or apron that was called a *nagua*. The length of the apron was dependent upon the woman's social status. Those women with the highest status wore the longest *naguas*.

Instead of clothing, the Amerindians decorated themselves with elaborate designs of red, white, and black pigments that were obtained from plants and vegetable dyes. The use of such face and body paint indicated many important things about an individual, including his or her sex and social status. The Carib also employed body painting as a way to intimidate their opponents during warfare.

The special clothing they wore during rituals and religious celebrations easily identified Taino chiefs and members of the nobility. This clothing was made of the finest woven cotton and featured beaded belts with geometric designs. The nobility often donned capes made from the colorful plumage of parrots, toucans, herons, or eagles.

All Amerindians, regardless of tribe, sex, or status, wore beautiful jewelry made from shells, gold, semiprecious stones, and bone. The gold for these ornaments was not mined. Instead gold nuggets were handpicked from rivers and streams. The gold was then pounded into foil strips for use in decorating ceremonial masks and jewelry.

Taino Farming

One of the reasons the Taino chose to settle in the Caribbean was the extremely fertile soil they discovered there. The availability of this good soil enabled the Taino to plant, cultivate, and harvest an abundance of crops. While the Carib planted small vegetable gardens, they were by no means the successful farmers that the Taino were.

The Taino's success as farmers was due to their creativeness and their ability to adapt to their environments. In fact, historians agree that the method of agriculture developed by the Taino was more efficient than anything the Europeans were using. Historian Kirkpatrick Sale elaborates: "It was highly productive, surpassing anything the Europeans could do at the time, with labor that amounted to hardly more than two or three hours a week. It was also a continuous year-long harvest. It offered the highest returns of food . . . by the simplest methods and modest labor."[6]

Farming Methods

Although the early Arawak had not been farmers, later Taino produced at least two yearly crops of several different vegetables. These included cassava, maize, potatoes, peanuts, peppers, beans, and squash. Initially, cultivation was done by the slash-and-burn method of agriculture that was common throughout the Caribbean and Central and South America. In this type of agriculture, the cultivated area was burned and abandoned after each harvest and the people moved on to a more fertile area.

Soon the Taino developed an even better method of producing rich harvests that was virtually maintenance free. This technique was based primarily on fields of knee-high mounds called *conucos,* which were planted with cassava, sweet potatoes, and various beans and squashes all grown together.

Historians explain this system: "They raised their crops in a conuco, a large mound which was devised especially for farming. They packed the conuco with leaves to protect from soil erosion and fixed a large variety of crops to assure that something would grow, no matter what weather conditions prevailed."[7]

The Indians worked the soil with sticks, called *coas,* and also used certain fertilizers like compost material. Archaeologists have also discovered evidence of simple irrigation techniques in parts of southwestern Hispaniola. Most of the labor was performed by the lower class with the men clearing the fields for farming and the women planting and cultivating the crops.

In addition to numerous nutritious crops, the Taino also grew cotton. The cotton was then spun into threads for hammocks and simple garments. Tobacco was another item that was widely grown by the Taino. The Amerindians rolled up a tobacco leaf, ignited it, and inhaled the smoke through their nostrils. Smoking was not only part

Cassava

Cassava, also called yucca or manioc, was the primary staple food of the Taino. It is a root crop from which a poisonous juice must be squeezed and removed. Cassava tubers, in fact, are loaded with prussic acid, an ingredient that is so poisonous that drinking the juice of raw roots was a traditional way of committing suicide.

Early on, however, the Taino learned to extract the poison from the cassava to produce edible food. This process involved cleaning the roots with a wooden knife, cutting the root into pieces, and leaving them in a bowl containing water and a piece of rotten cassava for twenty-four hours. This soaking caused the roots to soften and release their poison.

The soggy roots were grated on a bamboo board that had been pierced with palm thorns. The resulting substance was placed in a fiber press or squeezer whose upper part was hung from the branch of a small tree. A stick was then inserted into the lower part. A Taino woman usually sat on the thick stick to press down on the squeezer and expel the liquid poison. The remaining pulp was then dried in the sun and sifted through a wickerwork sieve to make flour. This flour was mixed with water and cooked into thin tortilla-like cakes called *cazabe*. The *cazabe* could be filled with meat, fish, and/or vegetables.

---

of their social life, but played a significant role in their religious ceremonies as well.

When Columbus landed on the island of Cuba in the late fifteenth century, he witnessed the Taino smoking tobacco. He described this practice in his journal: "On the way inland, my men found many people who were going to different villages, men and women, carrying firebrands in their hands and herbs to smoke."[8]

Hunting

There are few large mammals in the Caribbean. Because there was no land mass connecting the various islands to the mainland, the more sizable animals native to South and Central America were unable to migrate to the offshore lands. As a consequence, the only mammals that are found in the Caribbean are small ones such as rats, mice, and the *huiti,* a catlike rodent that gnaws on trees. These rodents probably arrived on the islands aboard driftwood.

The Taino and Carib Amerindians made wide use of those animals that were on the islands. In addition to rodents, snakes, lizards, and turtles were also caught and savored by the indigenous people of the area. Birds that migrated and lived on the islands were favorite prey, as well. The manatee, a large sea mammal then in plentiful supply, was also widely hunted.

The Manatee

The manatee or sea cow is a mammal that eats up to one hundred pounds of water plants a day using its upper lip, which is divided in half like a pair of pliers. Its front legs are shaped like paddles. Nearly thirteen feet long and weighing nearly thirty-five hundred pounds, manatees make their homes in the shallow coastal waters and rivers of the Caribbean and Florida.

The manatee was once widely hunted by both the Carib and the Taino Amerindi- ans of the Caribbean. The meat from this mammal could feed an entire village for several months, while the manatee skin could be used to make leather and rope. Even the manatee bones were useful. They were often carved into tools and various works of art.

Manatee numbers, worldwide, are now dropping rapidly due to loss of natural habitat and boating accidents. The animal is protected under the Endangered Species Act in the United States.

The meat from a manatee could feed an entire village for months.

Fishing

It was fishing, however, that provided the most food for the Caribbean's indigenous people. Most fishing was done along the coast and in the rivers found on the larger islands. Fish were abundant in these waters.

Many of the Amerindians fished using a net made of plant fibers or cotton. They also formed harpoons from wood and then tipped them with sharp points made from bone or shell. The Taino and the Carib also used bows and arrows and blowguns to kill fish. Blow- guns were small lengths of hollowed-out wood through which people blew a sharp dart-like projectile that was often dipped in poison.

The Taino, in particular, frequently used elaborate traps to catch fish. A woven z-shaped box was dropped overboard from a canoe so that it rested on the coral reef, seemingly offering a safe place for smaller fish to hide from various predators such as sharks. Fish swam inside the woven trap to check out their new home and were then unable to get out. No bait was needed for this technique, just patience on the part of the fishermen.

The Taino also caught fish by using a poison they extracted from a local vine. Historian Paul Reddish describes this technique: "A small section of a tributary is blocked off and the poison washed into the water. The fish soon appear on the surface, stupefied by the poison. The dying fish are then easily collected by the members of the village."[9] The poison was a quick-acting respiratory depressant that killed the fish through suffocation. Its effects were short-lived and rendered harmless before the fish were ingested by the Amerindians.

In addition, the Taino and Carib were able to locate large schools of tuna by watching the seabirds. Tuna feed on small fish that often swim in large groups. The seabirds also feed on these small fish. The indigenous fishermen simply watched where the birds were circling and diving and then headed their canoes in that direction.

Food and Cooking

Most of the Amerindians ate their fish or meat either raw or partially cooked. Fish

These boys proudly show off conches they have caught. A large mollusk, conch provided Amerindians with a steady source of meat, and today it is a delicacy in Caribbean cuisine.

were usually cooked by grilling on wooden stakes and served with a special sauce called *taumalin.* This sauce was made of lemon juice, pepper, and the green meat found inside the shell of a crab. Another favorite fish dish for both the Taino and the Carib was conch, a large shellfish that provided a dependable source of meat and protein. This giant mollusk lives in shallow grass beds along the shore. Conch, because of its lack of movement, was easy to gather and the shell was packed with meat. Conch is still relished today in the Caribbean and is considered a great delicacy.

The Taino relied far more on agricultural products than did the Carib. Food was generally prepared by baking it on stones or barbecuing it over an open fire. The Taino lavishly seasoned their food with peppers, herbs, and spices, not only to enhance the taste but to preserve certain food for later eating. According to writer Margaret Morris, one legacy of the Taino is "*bammy,* a thick pancake made from cassava [a root crop] and delicious fried with fish."[10] The Taino were also fond of a kind of stew called "pepper pot," made with cassava that was seasoned with meats, yams, sweet potatoes, and lots of pepper.

The Taino and other Caribbean Amerindians usually used gourds, called calabashes, for drinking water. These came from the *higuero* tree and, when hollowed out, made excellent containers. The indigenous people also used these gourds in their canoes for bailing purposes.

Regardless of where the Amerindians settled, there was a large variety of food available for consumption. As was true in many other areas of their lives, the Taino and Carib were able to utilize their resources well. In fact, their ability to adapt to their new island homes enabled the indigenous people of the Caribbean to evolve into rich and complex societies and cultures.

Chapter 2

Amerindian Society and Culture

It was not until the beginning of the twentieth century that archaeologists and historians became seriously interested in the indigenous cultures of the Caribbean. In fact, until recently the Taino and the Carib had been peripheral to the study of pre-Columbian societies. Scholars focused instead on the high cultures of Central and South America—the Aztec, Maya, and Inca.

Taino Society

While the Carib never achieved the complexity of the Taino, their society nonetheless evolved into a stable and unique culture that focused on warfare and expansion. Taino society, on the other hand, evolved into a number of complex political entities that resembled states.

The Taino were one of the most enigmatic of all the cultures of Central America and the Caribbean. "They left no great temples or other masterpieces of architecture as did the Maya," writes historian Paul Reddish. "They had no writing . . . and worst of all, within ten decades of Columbus' arrival, the Taino people tragically slipped out of the historic period."[11]

Journalist Michael D. Lemonick, however, cautions against drawing the wrong conclusion about Taino culture: "But it is a mistake to assume, as many scholars have until recently, that the absence of artifacts meant the Taino were necessarily more primitive than the grander civilizations of Central and South America. They simply used less durable materials."[12] Lacking the sources of limestone and granite available on the mainland, the Taino built with wood, not stone. In addition, through their wide-ranging trading contacts with these other civilizations, the Taino were able to adopt many Mesoamerican and South American cultural traits into their own society.

The Class System of the Taino

Taino society was characterized by a clear division of the people into different classes. The upper class or elite was called the *ni-taino*. These individuals were members of

Appearance

The Carib were a strong and muscular people slightly shorter than Europeans of the time. Unlike the Taino who had short hair, the Carib had straight long black hair that was worn loose. They were also clean-shaven because the Carib believed that beards and facial hair were deformities.

Both groups of Amerindians painted their brown skin with a vegetable dye called *roucou*. The Carib also disfigured their cheeks with deep incisions and hideous scars, which they stained with black, and they painted white and black circles round their eyes. These scars and other body decorations were believed to make the Carib warriors look fierce.

Many of the Amerindians also perforated the cartilage that lies between the nostrils and then inserted the bones of fish, a parrot feather, or even a fragment of a turtle shell. They wore bracelets and necklaces made out of amber, shell, animal teeth, seeds, coral, and even the teeth of their dead ancestors. Their ears and lips were also pierced and they generally used smooth fish bones and other ornaments to dangle from these areas.

The Carib and the Taino frequently wore small religious amulets around their necks. On a few special occasions the nobility and caciques wore feathered head-dresses.

the nobility and their numbers included the chiefs, warriors, rulers, artisans, religious leaders, and craftsmen of Taino society.

The lower class, called *naboria,* was composed of two separate social divisions. The first of these divisions included the commoners or ordinary people. These individuals resided in the smaller villages surrounding the large dwelling compounds of the elite. They often lived in the open country near the fields they were responsible for cultivating. Many were fishermen who lived near the shore. These individuals paid a tribute to the *nitaino* in the form of fish and game or the crops they raised in the cultivated fields.

The second division of the lower class was composed of the destitute, who were primarily the servants of the elite. While not quite slaves, this group of people performed most of the hard labor in Taino society.

Chiefs or Caciques

Taino society was governed by a hierarchy of greater and lesser chiefs known as caciques. All caciques were members of the *nitaino* class and were advised by other high-ranking nobles and priests. The Taino had a matriarchal society which meant that all village chiefs inherited their position through the female line. When a cacique died, for instance, his sister's son, rather than his own, succeeded him.

Each village had its own cacique, but these individual chiefs were often under the leadership of a higher or more powerful cacique who ruled in times of war or conflict. This greater cacique ruled over the *cacicazgo,* a confederation of communities with populations that ranged from several hundred to thousands of people. As Taino society matured between 1200 and the arrival of the Europeans, powerful caciques were able to unite these villages into political states.

Role of the Cacique in Taino Society

Caciques often formed political alliances through marriage, often marrying women of the elite or ruling class from neighboring villages. As a result of these marriages, conflict between rival tribes was often avoided.

Taino chiefs were usually well supplied with wives. While nearly every Taino man had two or three wives, the cacique often had as many as thirty. It was considered a great honor for a woman to be married to a cacique. Not only did she enjoy a materially superior lifestyle, but her children were held in especially high esteem.

The caciques had total power over every aspect of Taino society. Historian Alvin M. Josephy Jr. explains: "[The caciques controlled] the production and distribution of most of the necessities of life, including

Caciques, like the one pictured here, wore elaborate headpieces to denote their stature as chief. Caciques controlled nearly every facet of Taino society.

food, utensils for farming, fishing, and domestic needs, and the little clothing that the people wore in the warm, humid islands. In times of warfare, they also led the chiefdom's fighting men."[13]

Caciques were also responsible for organizing the yearly celebrations, known as *areytos,* that were held to honor the ancestors. It was also the caciques who decided if and when to go to war, and they frequently served as spiritual leaders who, the people believed, were able to contact the supernatural world through the use of hallucinogenic drugs.

The cacique generally wore a distinctive headpiece, often a cotton band that was decorated with gold. It was also adorned with parrot feathers in many different bright colors. Caciques carried ornately carved scepters and daggers of polished stone as symbols of their authority. Furthermore, caciques were frequently carried on a litter by the *naborias,* especially during special ceremonies or festivities.

Class System of the Carib

For the most part, the Carib class and social system was much simpler than that of the Taino. According to historian Franklin W. Knight, "the social and political organization of Carib society reflected both their military inclination and their mobile status."[14]

There were no chiefs or caciques in Carib society. Rather, the head of the family usually served as the leader of a village. He was responsible for food gathering and fishing and also for organizing the cultivation of crops. In addition, this informal leader also settled internal disputes and led raids against neighboring groups. This

Amerindian Family Life

The wealth and power of a Carib man was determined by the size of his family. As a result, women were of special value in that they were the ones who produced children. The primary reason for many of the raids made by the Carib was, in fact, to obtain wives for the young unmarried males in the village. This practice was known as "bride capture." The Carib believed that there was nothing more valuable to be bought, traded, or stolen than women.

Parents usually arranged marriages in Amerindian society, with girls and boys usually marrying between the ages of sixteen and eighteen. Women were expected to have many children, while those women who, for whatever reason, could not have children were considered a disgrace. Even more of a disgrace was a woman who committed adultery. If a woman was found to have done so, she was usually put to death.

headman was called a *tiubutuli hauthe*. Compared with the Taino cacique, he had little real authority.

The Role of Warfare in Carib Society

Before the arrival of the Spanish, the Carib were the most feared warriors of the Caribbean. Warriors were highly respected in Carib society, with every male expected to participate in raids and battles. In fact, according to journalist Carleton Mitchell, "The making of a Carib warrior began at birth. As soon as a male child was brought into the world, he was sprinkled with some drops of his father's blood."[15] The Carib believed that this practice transmitted a father's courage to his son.

As each boy grew older, his education consisted primarily of preparing him to become a good warrior. For instance, he learned at an early age to make and use weapons. "One method of making their boys skillful . . . in the exercise of the bow," writes Carleton Mitchell, "was to suspend their food on the branch of a tree, compelling the . . . [boys] to pierce it with their arrows before they could obtain permission to eat."[16] As the children grew older, the items were placed farther and farther away.

Unsurprisingly then, warfare played an important and pivotal role in Carib culture. "From their strongholds in St. Vincent and Dominica," writes journalist Peter T. Muilenburg, "the Carib warriors issued forth in their great war dugouts eager for battle, women, and loot."[17] By the time of the Spanish arrival in the New World, the Carib had conquered most of the Lesser Antilles region of the Caribbean.

Carib War Preparations

Prior to embarking on a raiding expedition, the Carib elders chose a war leader or *ubutu*. The *ubutu* had to be a good warrior who had proven his strength and bravery during a previous battle. While the position of a *ubutu* was usually temporary, it could become permanent if an upcoming raid was successful.

The *ubutu* was responsible for choosing the day and time of each attack. Once this day had been announced, each Carib warrior would collect a stick and make notches on it in order to count the days until the actual time of attack. To further prepare for battle, each warrior painted himself in vivid red, white, and black colors.

Most raids were made under the cover of night and were initially fought from large dugout canoes. The attacks were always sudden and brutal, often starting with a shower of fire arrows that were launched onto the thatch-roofed houses of the enemy. When people ran out of their burning houses, the Carib disembarked from their canoes and attacked men, women, and children with war clubs and bows and arrows.

In addition to their war clubs made of bone, wood, and stone, the Carib applied a poison made from the sap of the manchineel tree to the tips of their arrows. This poison was powerful enough to kill a grown man if it came in contact with even a small scratch. The Carib also used wooden swords and knives sharpened to a fine point.

A cacique approaches Christopher Columbus in this depiction of Columbus's arrival in the Caribbean.

Carib warriors were awarded medals, called *caracolis*, for special courage. The Carib often took prisoners and sang songs of triumph as they sailed back home. They also strung together the teeth of any enemy who had been slain in battle and then wore them as anklets, bracelets, and armbands as symbols of success.

Raising Children

Although Spanish explorers who encountered fierce Carib tribesmen recorded de-tails of their fighting equipment and techniques, there is little information available about how the indigenous people of the region raised their children.

Historians do know that cranial deformation, a practice in which a child's head was intentionally reshaped, was the norm for Carib children. According to historian Manuel Lucena Salmoral, "The only reason for this custom would seem to have been one of aesthetics and the result was a head of remarkable shape. Splints were tied to the front and back of the head with string or straps, forcing the skull to grow upward."[18] The result was a boxlike look and a flattening of the head. The Carib believed that this facial shape was noble, handsome, and pleasing to the gods. They usually began the procedure in the first few days after birth.

Cranial deformation was also the norm in Taino society, apparently for the same reason attributed to the Carib. According to writer Margaret Morris, "They altered the shape of their heads by depressing their skulls in childhood with a wooden frame."[19]

Although Taino families lived together under one roof, in Carib society the men

Roles of Men and Women

Men and women played very different roles in Amerindian society. Taino men, for instance, cleared the fields for farming, hunted and fished, built canoes, and protected the village as needed. Taino women did virtually everything else. They cooked, tended to the needs of the family, worked in the fields, and harvested the crops. They also made pots, grills, and griddles from river clay and were responsible for raising the Taino children.

Men and women also played very different roles in Carib society. Men were expected to be warriors, priests, leaders, craftsmen, hunters, and builders, while Carib women, like their Taino counterparts, did everything else.

These roles were described by an unidentified early observer in an article by writer Kim Johnson entitled "The Taino" on the *Race and History* website:

"The men only hunt, fish and cut down trees. . . . The women have to do everything else. When the men return from

hunting, they just throw their game down in the doorway . . . and the women pick it up and cook it; or if they come back from their fishing, they leave the fish in the canoe. . . . The women have to run down to the canoe to get the fish and cook it at once, for they are expected to know that the fishermen are hungry."

Taino women make bread. Amerindian women were responsible for cooking, raising children, and tending to the home.

Child's Play

The game of *guamajico* is still played today by the Taino in the mountains of Puerto Rico. In this game, children squat around a three-foot circle with their *guamajicos*, which are made from the seeds of the algaroba and or *guama* trees. These large seeds are tied to a cord called a *jico*. The *guamajicos* are all placed within the center of the circle while each child holds onto the cord attached to his or her seed.

One child is picked to go first. That child takes his or her *guamajico* and swings down into the circle trying to strike and break the other players' seeds. If a child's seed breaks, he or she is out of the game. The next child then has a turn and play continues around the circle. The winner is the child with the last unbroken seed.

lived separately from their wives in a house called a *carbet*. Each individual wife had her own home, usually a simple hut. Female children in Carib society were expected to live with their mothers and learn those tasks that would prepare them to be good wives. Carib boys, on the other hand, lived with their mothers only until the age of four, at which time they moved in with their fathers. The Carib believed that the young boys would grow up "too soft" if they stayed with their mothers.

Most Carib boys were trained to become warriors but a few were selected for the

priesthood. These boys served as apprentices to an older priest or shaman until attaining enough maturity to accept a spiritual role in Carib society.

Leisure Time

The Taino and Carib lived busy lives tending the fields, hunting, fishing, and, in the case of the Carib, preparing for war. Despite the multiplicity of tasks, both groups of indigenous people found time for social gatherings and games.

The Taino, in particular, were a fun-loving people who engaged in a number of games played by both children and adults. The game for which they are most noted, however, is *batey,* a ball game that can be traced back to around 3000 B.C. and has its roots in Mexico.

According to the present-day Jatibonicu Taino Tribal Council of Puerto Rico, "The batey game was played by Taino tribes of the Greater Antilles and was an important inter-tribal social gathering event for all the families who would come to take part in the annual games."[20] The games were also played to work out any hostilities that might arise over territorial disputes.

Batey was played in a high-walled court using a hard, bouncy ball made from the rubber reed plant. Two teams of twelve individuals competed against each other. Special players called goalies tried to stop the ball from passing or hitting their stone backrest or goal. Each team attempted to carry the ball from their side of the court to the other. The *batu* or ball could also be bounced off

28

the surrounding stone walls of the *batey* ball court. This ball court was a paved area often lined with carved stones and usually located in the center of the village.

The players could not touch the ball with their hands. As in modern soccer, it was kept in the air by hitting it with the head, shoulders, arms, hips, legs, and feet. Unlike a soccer ball, however, the *batey* ball was quite heavy and could cause severe injury to anyone who was struck in an unprotected place. The Taino players wore a kind of partial body armor. Historians write: "The pre-Columbian ball game was potentially lethal because the solid balls . . . were heavy and extremely fast. Players wore protective belts and padded accessories on their arms and legs."[21]

One form of body armor was a stone belt or *yuke* worn around the waist to give a player a hard surface off which to bounce the *batu*. In addition to their protective nature, the belts also had religious significance and were carved with religious motifs.

Ceramics and Carving

Not much of the great artistry of the indigenous people of the Caribbean has survived to modern times. There are, however, excellent examples of Taino ceramics, jewelry, weaving, carving, and other artifacts in museums around the world. In addition, historians agree that the Carib were noteworthy for their basket weaving, an art that is being reintroduced among the Amerindians today.

The Taino played batey *in ball courts like this one.* Batey *was played as a form of recreation and was also an important social activity.*

The Taino were the most artistically advanced of the indigenous people of the Caribbean. Pictured here are Taino animal carvings.

The Taino were perhaps the most culturally advanced of all the indigenous groups who made the Caribbean their home. One of the hallmarks of their culture was pottery. "Taino pottery," write historians, "reached an expressionistic level comparable to that of the most advanced ceramic cultures on the mainland."[22]

The Taino used the rich soil on the islands to make remarkable ceramic pots and artifacts. To strengthen the pottery, the clay was mixed with sand, ash, vegetable fibers, and even crushed seashells. The Taino used the coil method. This method involves laying strips of wet clay vertically in concentric circles for making cups, jars, and bowls. To make plates or other flat-bottomed vessels, the coils were laid out in a horizontal fashion. The vessels were then smoothed by hand. When thoroughly dried, groups of ceramic pots and other vessels were fired together in large open fire pits.

In addition to ceramic work, the Taino were also well skilled in the carving of wood. Wood was carved into a variety of household articles as well as into spears that were used in self-defense. Wood was also used to make musical instruments.

Women played a significant role in Taino culture as artists. According to historians, "Sixteenth century accounts report that [women] wove costumes and hammocks, made ceramic vessels for food preparation and feasting, and commissioned and owned duhos, the ceremonial seats used by caciques, nobles, and shamans."[23]

The Carib, on the other hand, concentrated their efforts on basket weaving, and Carib women taught their daughters to weave at a very early age. Long, thin leaves, which had been cut into strips, were left to dry for up to two weeks until they had turned brown. The leaves were then soaked in mud until they turned a rich black color. It generally took the women only one day to weave a large basket that could be used for storing and carrying things.

The Indigenous Legacy

Neither the Carib nor the Taino had a written language. They did, however, make wide use of petroglyphs, symbols carved into the walls of caves and rocks. These drawings were often their sole means of written communication. Archaeologists have discovered many fine examples of this art on various islands of the Caribbean.

Words taken from the indigenous languages have become a common part of the English language. For example, *hurricane* comes from *huracán*, *canoe* from *canoa*, and *hammock* from *hamac*. And the entire island area is named for the Caribs.

The Amerindian legacy of the Carribean survives today. It lives on, not only in the words borrowed from their languages, but in the many indigenous customs that are still practiced in the Caribbean.

Chapter 3

Amerindian Spirituality and Religion

The indigenous people of the Caribbean perceived the world and everything in it as alive, including such features of the landscape as mountains, trees, the ocean, rivers, and caves. They believed that the spirit world controlled all aspects of their life and that this world was full of supernatural beings who resided in the world around them and in the souls of animals and people.

"It is the mythical and spiritual world," writes author Paul Reddish, "that informs the Taino of their culture and its customs."[24] Historian Alvin M. Josephy Jr. agrees: "A magic, marvelous universe of beliefs and ceremonies was at the core of everything these island people did and thought."[25] Almost everything the Amerindians did reflected their spirits, myths, and religious beliefs.

Basic Beliefs

The Taino and the Carib believed that every individual had a special relationship with the world around them, especially the animals and plants that played such an im-portant role in their ways of life. The most important belief they followed was that of maintaining a healthy relationship and balance with their gods and spirits. These spirits could be either beneficial or destructive.

The Amerindians believed, for instance, that a person could not take something away from the environment without then making some kind of a sacrifice in the form of seeds, tobacco, or good works. The Taino prior to, during, and after the cultivation of their crops, for example, performed religious rituals to thank the land and the gods for a bountiful harvest.

The indigenous people also believed that if a person was greedy or showed disrespect to the world, such behaviors would anger and upset the spirits. In retaliation, the spirits might make that person ill or bring misfortune to him, his family, or the entire community.

Both the Taino and the Carib believed in many spirits and gods. The spirits that presided over their lives included a creator god and many other gods and goddesses.

These spirits were associated with rain, wind, the sea, the successful growth of crops, health, and human fertility.

One of the most important deities for the Taino was *Atabey,* the goddess of fresh water and fertility. She was the mother of *Yucahu* (also known as *Yocahu*) who was the lord of the cassava tree and the god of the sea. "The Taino called their supreme being Yocahu," writes historian Salmoral. "He lived in the sky and gave them yucca [or cassava] to feed them. They could not address him directly but had to do so through the *zemi,* or small idols made of wood or stone in which he lived."[26]

Taino Gods and Intermediaries

Zemis were spirit intermediaries between the Taino and their supreme god. There were, for instance, *zemis* that dealt with weather and also those that governed crops. The *zemis* controlled various functions of the universe in much the same way the Greek and Roman gods did.

The *zemis* were often represented by statues or icons of wood, stone, bone, or human remains. These came in all shapes and sizes but were often three-pointed stones. Over time the Taino *zemis* became larger and more elaborate and often had faces of humans and animals sculpted on them. Many were adorned with semiprecious stones or gold. These *zemis* were kept in shrine rooms or on special altars in the home.

Each adult Taino usually carried a *zemi* in the form of a fetish, which is a small object believed to have special powers. They believed that being in the good graces of their *zemis* protected them from all sorts

Carib Healing

The Carib often attributed illness, death, and losses on the battlefield to a spell or hex from an enemy *maboya.* In response, a shaman or *boyez* was called upon to carry out some kind of a healing ceremony.

If a person was ill, for example, that individual's house was given a thorough cleansing. Gifts of fruit or cassava were placed on a special table called a *matoutou* and offered to the *maboya.* This *matoutou* was placed at one end of the room while family members sat on stools at the other end of the hut.

A *boyez* then entered the home and began singing special chants to call on the patient's gods, spirits, and ancestors. The *boyez* then struck the ground three times with his left foot. He smoked tobacco and then rubbed his hands in the smoke and waved it into the air five different times. The *boyez* then took the tobacco and broke it into five pieces, which were sprinkled on the patient. Following this ritual, the patient was given a special mixture of herbs to drink.

The Amerindians depicted in this woodcut are participating in a religious ceremony. The gods of the Taino and the Carib influenced every aspect of their daily lives.

of calamities, including disease, storms, or disaster in war.

In addition, each tribe kept special *zemis.* A fertility *zemi,* for instance, was often buried each time a crop was planted. The Taino believed that in doing this the *zemi* god would increase the harvest. The Taino also served cassava or manioc bread to the *zemis* as well as beverages and tobacco.

The Carib held similar beliefs to that of the Taino. Their main deity was called the *maboya.* The Carib believed that this being controlled everything in the world around them. Individual *maboya* figures, worn as amulets around the neck, were believed to help ward off evil spirits.

Shamans

The role of the shaman or medicine man was a central one in both Taino and Carib society. Called *bohikes* (or *behiques* or *bohiques*) in Taino society and *boyez* in the Carib world, the shamans were usually older men whose words of wisdom were listened to and obeyed. Their power, the Amerindians believed, came from their ability to communicate with the spirit world in an attempt to intercede with the gods on behalf of their people. Historians explain: "Only those in touch with the supernatural realm could heal the sick, predict the future, ensure the fertility of the world, and resolve the larger problems of existence."[27]

The indigenous people believed that, during the creation of the world, the gods covered the Earth with invisible layers of geometric designs. Destructive spirits who ripped holes in this covering, the Amerindians believed, caused illness, bad crops, and natural disasters such as hurricanes. The shaman's responsibility was to journey to the spirit world to repair these holes.

In Taino society, the *bohike* was also responsible for officiating at the puberty rites of young girls. At these rituals, he pleaded with the spirit world to bring fertility and many children to each of the girls.

The shaman's power as a healer also came from his ability to discover what spirits were causing illness. To bring harmony and health, the shaman needed to contact the of-fending spirit and somehow appease it. Throughout the ancient Americas, shamans often relied on hallucinogens or mind-altering substances to connect with the spirits of the otherworld for the purpose of healing.

The Use of Hallucinogens

Natural hallucinogens were regarded as sacred and always believed to have magical powers. Their preparation and ingestion were associated with elaborate rituals in Amerindian society. They were consumed only by those individuals believed to possess the ability to communicate with the spirits who dwelled in the otherworld.

The Taino and Carib were among many Amerindian groups who induced mind-altering experiences by means of *cohoba,* a

Carib Initiation Ceremony for Young Boys

An initiation ceremony took place when Carib boys were considered to be at a transitional stage between boyhood and manhood.

When a boy reached his twelfth birthday, he was seated on a stool in front of all the tribe's warriors. First, the boy's father explained what the young man's responsibilities and duties would be as an adult warrior in Carib society. Then the other warriors took a live bird and beat it against the boy's body until the bird was dead. In the process of this beating, the bird usually bit the boy repeatedly. The boy was then scratched all over his torso with the bird's sharp claws and teeth. Finally, he was rubbed down with a pepper extract. This process was extremely painful but the Carib expected each young man to bear it without complaining.

The boy was then given the bird's heart to eat. Following these practices, the boy was led to his hammock where he was told to abstain from food or drink for a certain period of time. After this fasting, the young man was given a warrior's name and was permitted, for the first time, to go on enemy raids with the warriors.

drug that was prepared by grinding the seeds of certain trees native to South America and the Caribbean. The effects of *cohoba* are mainly visual. According to historians, the drug causes the user to "see the world in an inverted way: people, animals and objects appear upside down; movements and gestures are reversed; and perceptions are marked by constantly shifting shapes and kaleidoscopic colors."[28]

Before ingesting the *cohoba,* the shamans fasted and purged themselves with what students of ancient cultures call a vomiting spatula, a semiflexible length of wood and bone that causes one to gag when inserted down the throat. It was necessary to purge oneself, the indigenous people believed, in order for them to be pure and untainted on their journeys to the spirit world.

After vomiting as much as possible, the shaman inhaled the *cohoba* that had been mixed with tobacco in order to maximize its effects. In Taino society, the *bohike* sat on his *duho* with his elbows resting on his knees, his body hunched forward, and his mind focused on the thoughts and images that would follow. In this position, the *bohike* was best able to communicate with the spirits and the ancestors.

Religious Ceremonies in Taino Society

Shamans were also responsible for formal religious services that helped the Taino maintain a healthy balance between the spirits of destruction and harmony. These ceremonies were held to enlist the help of the gods and goddesses that controlled their world and also to acknowledge the spirits' powers.

The Taino wore special clothing for these ceremonies. They would generally cover themselves from the knees down with shells and other ornaments, while also wearing brightly colored paint and feathers.

The *bohike* began by presenting the cacique with ornate carved figures of the community's major *zemis*. On a *duho* in a special place of honor, the cacique presided over the service, which began with a ceremonial beating of the drums. Women then served special bread, first to the *zemis* and then to the cacique, before serving the entire group. The bread was followed by an oral history lesson during which there was the singing of epic songs which honored the cacique and the ancestors.

Deaths and Funerals in Taino Society

Despite the healing powers of the shamans and the spiritual benefits of religious ceremonies, death was an ever present factor in the lives of the indigenous people of the Caribbean. Both the Carib and the Taino believed in an afterlife. For the Taino, this afterlife was a place of great peace and harmony. To speed the dead on the way to their eternal homes, offerings and food as well as their important possessions were usually buried with their bodies. In addition, when a cacique died, one or more of his favorite wives was given a sleeping potion and buried alive with him.

The Taino, who were ancestor worshippers, believed that the spirits of the dead

Celebrations and Festivities in Taino Society

At the yearly celebrations called *areytos,* the Taino honored their ancestors and celebrated certain events in Taino life. The word *areyto* in the Taino language means "to recall." And that is what these festivals did—they recalled ancient traditions and celebrated victories, births, and bountiful crops. The *areytos* also had a religious and political overtone as they served to settle many territorial disputes without the shedding of any blood.

The primary activities at an *areyto* were singing and dancing. Many of the ancient traditions were sung at these feasts. Spanish chronicler Gonzalo Fernandez de Oviedo y Valdes told of the key role of these *areyto* songs. "Their songs, in those they called the areytos," he wrote in the late fifteenth century, as recounted in Alvin M. Josephy Jr.'s book *America in 1492*, "are their books and memorials, transmitted from generation to generation, from fathers to sons. . . . Thanks to their areytos they could recall [and celebrate] things of their past."

The singing was often accompanied by reed fifes and percussion or rhythm-making instruments. The Taino created percussion instruments from various gourds. These included maracas or gourd rattles and a long hollow gourd played with a stick, called a guiro. These two instruments are still played in the Caribbean today. They also used an instrument called a *mayohaboa*. This was a kind of drum made out of wood and then hollowed out.

Special food was also served during the *areytos*. Roasted iguana was usually served along with cassava bread, yams, pineapples, and corn beer. Mock battles and ball games were held between neighboring groups.

Taino tribesmen dance and play maracas at the areyto *depicted here.*

remained in their bones and thus usually buried the dead under the homes of the families. The caciques and other high-ranking nobles, however, were usually given special funeral rites. After exposure to the elements, their skulls and long bones were cleaned and preserved in carved wooden urns or large calabash gourds which were then hung from the rafters of their former homes.

Deaths and Funerals in Carib Society

When a Carib Amerindian died, he or she was examined by the *boyez*. If the shaman determined that sorcery was the cause of death, he performed a special ritual to rid the body of evil spirits. The body was then carefully washed and painted red, while the hair was oiled and combed.

A grave, six feet deep and generally round, was usually dug into the floor of the house the dead person had lived in. The body was placed in the grave sitting up on a stool. A fire was built around the grave to keep the bugs away while, for ten days, relatives brought food and water to the corpse.

At the end of the ten-day period, the hole was filled. Following this, there was a special ceremony, during which the family and community danced around and over the grave. As a sign of mourning, each Carib relative was expected to cut off his or her hair. The deceased person's belongings were burned to prevent evil spirits from returning from the spirit world.

Occasionally, the Carib buried the bones of the dead in a large funeral urn that was sealed with a special stopper and decorated with drawings of human faces. The Amerindians often kept the skulls and bones of their loved ones, believing that these would bring good fortune.

Decorated with drawings of human faces, this gravestone marked the final resting place of an Arawak man.

Superstitions About Death

The Taino believed that the souls of the dead resided in the otherworld but returned to Earth each night. Thus, night-flying creatures such as owls and bats were regarded as messengers of the spirits. It was taboo, or forbidden, for any Taino to walk in the forest during the night. This, according to Reddish, "was because the spirits of the dead were active at night. . . . The day was the world of the living, the night the place of the dead."[29]

The Carib were also a superstitious people. For instance, if they were carrying fresh water in their canoes on long voyages, they made sure that none of this water spilled out into the ocean. They believed that if this happened, the gods would be angry and cause a bad storm to occur. On the other hand, if they were passing over an area of the sea where a fellow Carib had drowned, they often threw water into the sea in the hope that the dead man's spirit would not cause their boat to capsize.

Superstitions in the Caribbean Today

Many people of the Caribbean today are just as superstitious as the Amerindians of the past. Current superstitions, in fact, often originated with the indigenous people of the region. Others are combinations of Amerindian beliefs and those of other cultures.

People in the Caribbean today fear *duppies* who, like the spirits of the past, roam at night. In modern society, people hang herbs in their windows and doorways to prevent the *duppies* from entering their homes. They also scatter sand around their homes, a practice aimed at keeping the spirit occupied by counting each grain of sand until daylight comes.

The indigenous people of the Caribbean blamed illness, bad luck, and even death on evil spirits. These bringers of misfortune find their form today in loup-garous, spirits that were once human and whose souls were eaten by demons. Like the evil spirits that plagued the islanders of earlier times, loup-garous are blamed for everything bad that happens: illness, business failures, unfaithful boyfriends.

In the Dominican Republic, where the Taino once thrived, it is believed that pregnant women must not eat fruit or coconut. To do so, some people believe, will cause the baby not to breathe properly. Another folk belief is that if a pregnant woman lifts her arms over her head, the fetus might strangle on the umbilical cord.

Cannibalism in Carib Society

Were the Carib really cannibals as the Spanish believed? Although most historians agree that there is little evidence to support this claim, many Caribbean school textbooks perpetuate it.

These texts, according to writer Franklin W. Knight, report that "using bows, poisoned arrows, javelins, and clubs, the Carib attacked in long canoes, capturing Arawak women and, according to Arawak informants, ritualistically cooking and eating some of the male captives." Knight continues,

Carib Amerindians are shown cooking a human body in this drawing by a European explorer. Amerindians consumed parts of fallen enemies as ceremonial ritual.

however, by stating that there are "no records of Carib eating humans."[30]

National Geographic writer Robert Booth visited the Carib community on the island of Dominica in the early 1990s and spoke at length to chief Irvince Auguiste. "There may have been ritual use of enemy remains," acknowledges Auguiste, "but we have no tradition, no oral history of cannibalism."[31]

The "ritual use of enemy remains" was common throughout the New World. The Carib, like many of their neighbors, believed that by consuming parts of enemy warriors, they could gain possession of dead enemies' or ancestors' souls and noteworthy qualities. Historian Reddish elaborates: "Caribs ate parts of fallen enemies mainly as a ceremonial ritual. This was done to capture the spirit and power of the enemy."[32]

A Dire Prediction

Both the Carib and the Taino centered their lives around their spiritual beliefs. These beliefs, along with their customs and simple ways of life, allowed both groups of indigenous people to thrive in relative harmony on the islands of the Caribbean for many centuries. This harmony was to be severely threatened in the late fifteenth century with the arrival of an Italian explorer named Christopher Columbus.

This arrival of a strange people had been prophesied many years earlier by a Taino shaman. One of the Taino gods had led the shaman to believe that the Taino "would enjoy their domain for only a brief period of time," writes historian Alvin M. Josephy Jr., "before 'dressed people,' [who looked] very different, [would] come to their land and . . . impose themselves [upon the tribe]."[33]

Chapter 4

The Discovery of the New World

On the eve of explorer Christopher Columbus's voyage to the Americas in 1492, more than 4 million Amerindians—Lucayans, Taino, and Carib—are estimated to have occupied the various islands of the Caribbean. Some historians believe this number may have been as high as 6 million.

"The arrival of Columbus on the shores of the Caribbean," writes historian Paul Reddish, "was to change the whole world."[34] And for people of the Caribbean, the Spanish expedition meant their near extinction.

Beginning with the Spanish and continuing later with other Europeans, the indigenous people of the Caribbean experienced a series of violent upheavals. According to Franklin W. Knight, "The European intrusion abruptly interrupted their pattern of historical development. . . . It also severely altered their physical environment, introducing both new foods and new epidemic diseases. As a result, the native Indian populations rapidly and [nearly] disappeared from the Caribbean."[35]

Christopher Columbus

Christopher Columbus is the English version of the name of Cristoforo Columbo, born in Genoa, Italy, in 1451. While little is known about the childhood of the future explorer, historians do know that, while a young man, Columbus supported himself as a mapmaker in Portugal.

Based on information he acquired during early travels to the Far East and by reading and studying his maps, Columbus concluded that the Earth was actually much smaller than geographers thought. In addition, he erroneously believed that the Earth was composed primarily of land, not water. On the basis of these two faulty conclusions, Columbus decided that he could reach Asia quickly merely by sailing west for a few days.

In 1484 Columbus presented his theories to King John II of Portugal and requested permission to set forth on a trip to Asia. His attempt to have the Portuguese king finance such a trip failed. Columbus then moved to Spain where he made several similar proposals to Queen Isabella I and King Ferdinand V of Castile, Spain. In 1492 he was finally given a fleet of three ships and the finances to outfit such a journey. According to Franklin W. Knight, Columbus aimed "to establish direct commercial relations with the producers of spices and other luxuries of the fabled East, thereby cutting out the Arab middlemen, who had monopolized trade."[36] He also hoped to discover and exploit vast riches of gold and other precious metals.

Voyage of Discovery

Columbus set sail with three ships on his voyage of exploration and discovery. The largest ship was the *Santa Maria,* a decked ship about one hundred feet long. The *Pinta* and the *Niña,* two smaller vessels of about fifty feet each, completed his small fleet. The entourage sailed on August 3, 1492, with a total complement of ninety men.

The crew shared Columbus's dream of finding riches and gold. "The men aboard also knew, each of them," writes historian Kirkpatrick Sale, "that for decades, perhaps centuries, mariners and geographers and travelers had told of places of fantastic wealth out there on the farther edge of the ocean, and there was every reason to suppose that those stories of golden cities and magical fountains and fist-sized jewels might well come true for them."[37]

After a brief stop in the Canary Islands off the coast of Spain for repairs to one of the ships, the fleet finally

sighted land again on October 12, 1492. They landed on the shores of an island in the Bahamas, called *Guanahani* by the indigenous people. Despite the fact that around forty thousand Lucayan natives occupied the land, Columbus claimed that, by right of conquest, their island now belonged to Spain. He then proceeded to rename the island San Salvador, meaning "Holy Savior."

During this first voyage, Columbus and his men thoroughly explored many other islands in the Bahamas and also visited Cuba and the island of Hispaniola. Columbus and his men all thought they were in Asian

Christopher Columbus explored Cuba, Hispaniola, and many islands in the Bahamas.

This painting depicts Christopher Columbus and his men landing on San Salvador in 1492. Columbus claimed the island for Spain even though Lucayan Indians were living there.

waters and named the entire area the West Indies. Because the name *Indian* comes from the mistaken belief of fifteenth-century Europeans that they were close to the country of India, indigenous people today point out that the term is inappropriate.

The Amerindians Greet the Newcomers

When Columbus landed on San Salvador, the Lucayans fled into the forest. Eventually, they were lured into the open, bringing with them parrots and cotton cloth that they traded for bright shiny European beads. Au-

thor Louise B. Young speculates that: "The Lucayans must have been filled with awe and wonder. They welcomed this new visitation with gifts of food and celebration, little suspecting that it would lead to the worst disaster they would ever suffer."[38]

Christopher Columbus was a great believer in keeping written records of his journeys. During his visits to the Caribbean he filled countless journals with his thoughts and observations. Columbus wrote the following about the first people he encountered: "They are the best people in the world and above all the gentlest. . . . They

The Bahamas

The Bahamas are a chain of seven hundred islands lying in the North Atlantic. They also include over two thousand rocky islets and cays—the word *cay* comes from the Amerindian word *cairi*, meaning island. Many of the islands remain uninhabited.

Christopher Columbus, during his first expedition to the New World, made landfall in the Bahamas. Despite the wide sandy beaches and abundance of vegetation, the Spanish did not settle this area of the Caribbean. The British finally claimed the islands on October 30, 1629. Early settlements failed due to the remoteness of the area.

The Bahamas, instead, became a pirate stronghold. The seventeenth century saw the islands being used by French and English pirates who used the strategic location to raid Spanish gold ships. The area was finally cleared of pirates in the early eighteenth century. The islands remained in British hands. Thousands of British citizens fled to the Bahamas following Great Britain's loss in the American Revolution. By the early 1800s the population of the islands had tripled.

The British continued to colonize the area and use the land for plantations and other profitable resources. In recent years the Bahamas have become one of the most important tourism areas in the Caribbean. In 1973 the islands were granted their independence from Great Britain, but remain today part of the British Commonwealth.

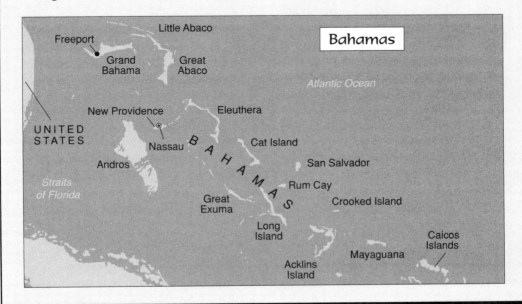

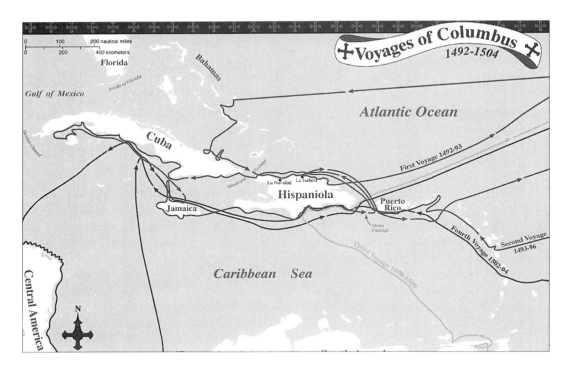

became so much our friends that it was a marvel. . . . They traded and gave everything they had, with good will. . . . They are . . . without knowledge of what is evil; nor do they murder or steal."[39]

Despite these words of praise, Columbus apparently had no reservations about using the Lucayans to serve his own purposes. In a letter written to the king and queen of Spain, Columbus reported: "When your Highnesses so command, they can all be carried off . . . or held captive on the island itself . . . [and] kept in subjection and forced to do whatever may be wished."[40] Columbus added: "They ought to be good servants. . . . I believe that they would easily be made Christians, because it seemed to me that they had no religion."[41]

La Navidad

The first structure erected by the Spanish in the New World was a fortress. It was built toward the end of Columbus's first trip to the Caribbean on the island of Hispaniola (now Haiti and the Dominican Republic) at a spot the Europeans called La Navidad. The fortress was built from timber salvaged from the *Santa Maria*, which had struck rocks and been stranded off the coast of the island. Noticing that the natives were wearing gold jewelry and hoping to find the source of the riches, Columbus left a small garrison of troops at La Navidad and sailed off to Spain to report his discoveries to Ferdinand and Isabella.

Upon his return to the outpost in November 1493 with a contingent of fifteen

Hispaniola

Hispaniola is the name the Spanish gave to one of the largest islands in the Caribbean. Christopher Columbus landed there in 1493, claiming the island on behalf of Spain. The first permanent settlement in the New World was originally named Isabella and formed at present-day Santo Domingo.

In the late sixteenth century, having extracted as much gold as they could on the island, the Spanish began losing their grip on Hispaniola. Hispaniola became little more than a way station between Spain and the conquered lands of Central and South America. The French moved in and took control of much of the island.

A revolution in the western part of the island led to the independence of the newly created Republic of Haiti in 1804. The eastern half was given its independence in February 1844 and took the name the Dominican Republic. The United States took an interest in the Dominican Republic in 1905. President Theodore Roosevelt sent American troops to the area to quiet the unrest that threatened the building of the nearby Panama Canal. The troops were able to stabilize the government before leaving the island in the 1920s.

Rafael Leónidas Trujillo Molina took control of the Dominican government in

President Rafael Leónidas Trujillo Molina controlled the Dominican government for more than thirty years.

February 1930 in a series of rigged elections. A corrupt and ruthless dictator who was assassinated in 1961, Trujillo is nonetheless still regarded as a father figure by the Dominican people. The first free elections in that country were held in 1962.

Today, two distinct cultures exist side by side on Hispaniola. Most of the people in both countries are poor, for the depredations of the Europeans left thus far insurmountable difficulties.

hundred men on seventeen vessels, Columbus found that the troops left behind had run out of control, abusing the Taino women, seizing the people's food supplies, and committing other offenses. An eyewitness, Spanish voyager Guillermo Coma, cited "the licentious conduct of our men towards the Indian women," reporting that "each Spaniard had five women to minister to his pleasure."[42]

Christopher Columbus kneels before King Ferdinand and Queen Isabella. The Spanish monarchs funded Columbus's voyages in hopes that his ships would return laden with gold.

Caonabo, a Taino cacique from southern Hispaniola, had retaliated by organizing a rebellion in which most of the men in the garrison at La Navidad were killed. The returning Europeans were quick to mount their own bloody retaliation, destroying the goodwill of the indigenous people and establishing a pattern of cruelty toward them that would have horrifying results.

To replace the ruined fortress at La Navidad, Columbus established the colony of Isabella (soon to be known as Santo Domingo) on Hispaniola and, with the explorer himself as the first governor, it became the first prolonged settlement of Europeans in the New World.

The Search for Gold

When Christopher Columbus returned to Spain after his first voyage of discovery, he carried with him a small amount of gold and fascinating accounts of the fabulously rich lands of the east. Thus the king and queen commissioned him to go back to the region they thought of as the West Indies to develop trade with the Amerindians, convert them to Christianity, and, most importantly, to find gold and other riches.

Accordingly, between 1494 and 1502, Columbus relentlessly sailed from one Caribbean island to another looking for gold. Historian Kirkpatrick Sale clarifies the European priorities during this period: "The Sovereigns might talk of religious conversion and the Admiral [Columbus] might talk of settlement . . . but the real purpose of colonization . . . was gold."[43]

The treasure, however, turned out to be more elusive than Columbus and the Spanish monarchs expected. While there were considerable deposits of gold in the mountains of Hispaniola, the difficult terrain there lessened the chances of success. Nevertheless, the Europeans persevered, forcibly enlisting the assistance of the Taino as their own hardships increased. The result, says writer Louise B. Young, was that "within two years the entire island of Hispaniola was turned into a brutal labor camp, with the Tainos forced to work long hours panning the riverbeds and digging in the mountains to locate deposits of gold."[44]

Enslavement of the Amerindians

Nobody was safe from the treasure seekers. Wherever they went the Europeans took prisoners and forced the Amerindians to work as slaves. Girolamo Benzoni was an Italian who participated in the raids made against the Caribbean Indians. In 1555 he made the following entry in his journal: "All along the coast, the Indians came down from the hills to the shore to fish. We, therefore, used to hide ourselves in places where we could not be seen. We often used to wait all day hoping to take prisoners. When the Indians arrived, we jumped out like wolves attacking so many lambs and made them slaves."[45]

Columbus, the Spanish, and the other Europeans who later settled in the Caribbean mercilessly exploited the peaceful indigenous people. When the slave ships visited the Bahamas, entire communities of Lucayans were forced into slavery. The captives, including children and the elderly, were crammed belowdecks where thousands died of starvation and disease before reaching Hispaniola. Once the

Spaniards mutilate Taino men and women in this drawing. Spanish conquistadors nearly wiped out the Taino population.

Lucayans arrived on Hispaniola, they were thrown into labor camps and treated abusively. Thousands more died until there were very few Lucayans left to enslave. By 1508 no Amerindians remained in the Bahama Islands.

Many historians believe that Columbus's use of the Amerindians was the beginning of slavery in the New World.

The Brutality of the Spanish

The violence that had marked early encounters between the Europeans and Amerindians escalated during Columbus's second and third visits to the Caribbean. Bartolomé de Las Casas, a Spanish priest who had been a slave owner, sailed to the New World as a missionary on Columbus's third expedition. He arrived at Santo Domingo on the island of Hispaniola in 1502. After spending several years in the Caribbean, Las Casas became a committed partisan of the Amerindians and frequently spoke out and wrote about the Spanish violence and abuse.

The reports of Las Casas have given modern scholars a vivid look at the period. "The Spanish," Las Casas wrote, "made bets as to who would slit a man in two. . . . They tore the babes from their mothers' breast by their feet and [then] dashed their heads against the rocks. . . . They burned the Indians alive."[46]

Las Casas was one of the very few contemporary observers to record genocidal acts by the Europeans in the Caribbean. "The island of Hispaniola," he wrote, "was the first to . . . suffer the wholesale slaughter of its people. . . . It all began with Europeans tak-ing native women and children. . . . They forced their way into native settlements, slaughtering everyone they found there, including small children, old men, pregnant women. . . . They hacked them to pieces."[47]

Although these atrocities occurred while Columbus was away from Hispaniola, the commander did not punish his men for these excesses when he returned in March 1495 to find the colony in turmoil. Rather, Columbus assembled over two hundred soldiers and equipped them with full armor and weapons. The group marched out to find any remaining Taino survivors. The result was a massacre. "The soldiers mowed down dozens," writes historian Kirkpatrick Sale, "loosened the dogs to rip open limbs and bellies, chased fleeing Indians into the bush to skewer them on swords . . . killing many Indians."[48]

When Columbus later learned that some of the Taino had also taken Spanish property, he ordered their noses and ears cut off and ultimately decided to have them beheaded.

The Taino Fight Back

The Taino were ill-prepared to fight back against the overwhelming numbers of Spanish. They were not a warlike people, nor did they train their young men to become warriors. They were peaceful farmers, utterly without resources to effectively respond to the brutality of the Europeans.

The Taino had no concept of war for the purpose of taking territory or destroying other peoples. Their simple weapons made of wood and stone were no match for the guns and cannons of the invaders.

In addition, the Taino beliefs led them to rely on spiritual rather than physical responses to aggression. "The Taino resistance [to the Spanish] was largely spiritual, depending on the cemis [*zemis*] of destruction to determine the fate of the Spanish invaders,"[49] writes historian Paul Reddish. As more and more of their people were enslaved and killed, many of the Taino came to the conclusion that their gods had abandoned them.

This is not to say that the Taino did not attempt to fight back but, in the end, their efforts were nearly meaningless. Las Casas recorded a story of individual bravery on the part of the Taino:

An Indian . . . rose in rebellion. . . . [He] was a courageous man [and] obtained a lance made of iron . . . [and] recruited ten or twelve Indians and with them began to attack the Spaniards in the mines, estates, or country farms, wherever they went in twos or fours or small groups. He killed all those he found, so that he spread panic, terror, and a strange fear throughout the island.[50]

Within a few years, Taino resistance had virtually disappeared. The Taino, who had helped Columbus and his men survive in the Caribbean, were repaid for their kindness by being abused, enslaved, and nearly exterminated at the hands of their guests.

The Beginning of Colonialism

With the Taino either eliminated or under the domination of the colonists, Christopher

The Tribute System

After his second voyage to the Caribbean, Columbus, now governor of Hispaniola, began to require the Taino to pay tribute to the Spanish crown. The Amerindians were expected to hand over a certain quantity of gold per person. Failing that, anyone over the age of fourteen had to submit twenty-five pounds of cotton.

To try to meet highly unrealistic demands, the Taino were forced to neglect their fields to pan for gold and raise cotton. Unable to raise enough crops to feed their own families, the Taino were soon suffering from malnutrition. Eventually famine swept through the Amerindian community.

By 1548 the Taino population, estimated in the millions in 1492, had been reduced to approximately five hundred. Not long thereafter, the Taino abruptly disappeared from the census records and the annals of history. They did not, as many historians believed, become extinct. Rather, they fled to the mountains, intermarried with blacks and Europeans, and fought to preserve themselves and their culture.

The Other Voyages of Columbus

After returning from his first voyage to the New World, Christopher Columbus was greeted enthusiastically by the king and queen of Spain. The monarchs, impressed with the discovery of new land, gave orders for Columbus to return and explore further.

The explorer left Spain in September 1493 on a second voyage of discovery, during which he made a landing on the island of Dominica. Hostile Carib warriors prevented any further exploration of that small island. Columbus went on to make landfall on many other islands of the Caribbean, including Puerto Rico, and once more returned to Spain. He set sail on his third voyage on May 30, 1498. He landed briefly on Trinidad but then returned to Hispaniola where he expanded the gold mining operations at Santo Domingo (the former Isabella, renamed in 1496).

In the meantime Columbus had made many enemies who were able to persuade the Spanish monarchs to replace him as governor of Hispaniola. He was arrested and returned to Spain in chains, but Ferdinand and Isabella eventually authorized his release and pardon.

Columbus did make a fourth voyage but he was forbidden to stop at Hispaniola. He instead sailed the waters off the coast of Central America and established a settlement in Panama. The explorer returned to Spain in November 1503 where the final months of his life were marked by illness and a vain attempt to secure his former privileges in the Caribbean. He was labeled a failure for never having found a way to India. He died May 20, 1506.

Columbus acted to solidify Spanish rule on the island of Hispaniola. Serving as governor of the island from 1495 to 1500, Columbus conceived a colonial policy for Spain that left a lasting imprint on life in the New World. This was the system of *repartimiento.*

Under the *repartimiento* system, each Spanish settler was granted a large tract of land along with any of the surviving Taino who lived on it. By 1500, however, abuse of the land and of the Amerindians led the Spanish king and queen to end this system and turn instead to the *encomienda* method. All the land, under this system, became the property of the crown, but the colonist to whom the land was granted was entitled to a certain amount of labor from native tenants.

In exchange the colonist was, in theory, responsible for looking after the physical well-being of the Amerindians. The Spanish in the New World were also charged with instructing the natives in Christianity. This system, planned by Europeans for their own benefit, allowed almost unlimited exploitation of the remaining Amerindians.

According to historian Kirkpatrick Sale, Spain's vision came "complete with conquest, religious conversion, city settlement, fortresses, exploitation [of the land and people], international trade and exclusive domain."[51] This model, which was adopted by other European countries as well, would ultimately lead to the complete colonization of the Caribbean and the continued enslavement and killing of the Caribbean Amerindians.

The Plantation System

The ceding of Caribbean land to European colonists under the *repartimiento* and *encomienda* systems set the stage for later developments in the region. Although modest amounts of gold were discovered and mined on the islands, the vast riches that the Spanish expected to find there never materialized. The Spanish would, instead, turn to Central and South America in their relentless search for gold.

In the Caribbean, the Spanish refocused their efforts and turned to ranching and the planting of sugarcane. Sugar was first planted in 1493 but large-scale plantations did not develop until well into the sixteenth century. By the second half of the seventeenth century, the plantation system had been well established.

The sugar industry changed the history of the Caribbean and the way people ate in Europe. Before settling this area, Europe had consumed very little sugar. The continent of Europe does not lend itself to the planting of this crop which grows only in warm, tropical climates. With the settlement of the Caribbean, sugar could be massively produced and harvested.

Sugarcane is a giant, thick, perennial grass cultivated for its sweet sap. The plant grows in clumps of solid stalks and has graceful sword-shaped leaves. Mature cane can grow to a height of ten to twenty-six feet and is nearly two inches in diameter. The colors range from almost white to yellow to deep green, purple, or red.

Sugar and its by-products of rum and molasses are still major exports in the Caribbean. Rum was first made in 1640 by distilling the juice extracted from molasses. Molasses is the thick liquid residue left after most of the sugar is taken out of sugarcane juice.

Large numbers of people were needed to work the sugarcane plantations. In the early colonial days, the Taino were forced to work the huge farms on the island of Hispaniola. From 1502 to 1509 colonial governor Nicolas de Ovando ruled Hispaniola with a harsh hand. He treated the Taino with brutality and the Amerindian population continued to rapidly decline. With the growing scarcity of Amerindians, a new labor force was required. Ovando began bringing in slaves from Africa.

The plantation system and the move toward the colonization of the Caribbean would have several lasting impacts on the Amerindians of the area. These effects would include the influx of African slaves along with the growth of several colonial empires.

Chapter 5

The Growth of Colonial Empires

The plantation system brought radical changes to the Caribbean and ultimately to the lives of the Amerindians who lived there. With the growing scarcity of native workers, a new labor force was needed. The Spanish and other colonial powers turned to the continent of Africa and began to import thousands of slaves.

Intermarriage with the Africans increased the numbers of indigenous populations and led to the formation of two separate groups who would resist further European expansion into the Caribbean. While this resistance would ultimately fail, it did slow down the settlement of the Lesser Antilles. Ultimately, attempts to colonize this area of the Caribbean would bring the Europeans into conflict with the warlike Carib.

African Slavery

Most of the slaves imported to the Caribbean came from western Africa. There, slave traders bought hundreds of thousands of people, often from their own leaders, and began the process of shipping them to the Americas. Conditions on the slave ships were appalling. The slaves were chained belowdecks where they lay for weeks, often months, side by side with no room to move and no access to fresh air. It is estimated that between 1510 and 1865 around 15 million men, women, and children were taken out of Africa and sent to the New World. It is also estimated that over one-fourth of these died before reaching the islands.

The slaves worked and lived in conditions that were nothing less than horrendous. European overseers and masters had total control over their charges. Revolts took place with increasing frequency. Slaves suffered terrible punishments at the hands of the Europeans, including nearly constant beatings and even killings. There are, for instance, reports of slaves being stuffed with gunpowder and then blown up. There are also reports of human body parts being chopped off for minor infractions and acts of disobedience.

Slavery was banned by the British in 1833, by the French in 1848, and by the United States in 1865. Cuba was the last Caribbean island to follow suit, giving up slavery in 1886.

Effect of African Slavery on the Taino

The influx of hundreds of thousands of African slaves had a dramatic effect on the lives of the surviving Amerindian populations. In parts of Hispaniola, Jamaica, Cuba, and other areas of the Greater Antilles, the blending of the two peoples led to the formation of a group of people called the maroons.

The name *maroon* comes from the Spanish word *cimarrón,* meaning "wild" or "un-tamed." Many West African slaves ultimately escaped their masters and fled into the mountains of Jamaica's interior. Recent archaeological excavations have produced evidence confirming maroon oral tradition that the escapees joined with the Taino and lived an isolated but free life. In time, the maroons came to control large areas of the Jamaican interior. Bands of maroons would, from time to time, swoop down from the hills to raid Spanish plantations.

The British moved into Jamaica in 1655 and seventy-five years later signed a treaty of peace that guaranteed the descendants of Africans the right to live unmolested in the Jamaica interior. Even after 1730, however, frequent treaty violations led to skirmishes between the two groups. The maroons were

Chained slaves are driven across a sugarcane field. European colonists imported slaves from Africa to replace the waning Taino population.

Voodoo Practices

Elaborate voodoo ceremonies are held in sacred places called *hounfors*. These sites can include anything from broken-down wooden sheds to vast clearings in the forest. In the center of the *hounfor* is an altar, called a *pe* or *sobagui*. Elaborately sewn flags provide the background.

Many of the flags are quite ornate and are made of silk or satin and embroidered with sequins, beads, pearls, and other ornamental items. At the beginning of a voodoo ceremony, the flags are taken from a secret hiding place and brought into the candlelight by the priest or priestess. The symbols on the flags are taken from several traditions—Taino, African, and European.

Among voodoo practitioners, there is a great celebration over the birth of a child. A newborn's umbilical cord is buried and a fruit tree is planted over the site. The tree and fruit will belong to that person throughout his or her lifetime.

Another feature of voodoo that reflects its African and Amerindian roots is the practice of "bush" medicine. Like their ancestors, voodoo practitioners use a variety of natural remedies to treat the sick and injured. Lemongrass and sage, for instance, are used to treat colds, while spiderwebs can be used over a cut to stop the bleeding. Peppermint tea is often given for nausea, while lime or Saint-John's-wort can be used for fever.

An ornately garbed voodoo spirit is depicted in this Haitian painting.

able to hold off the British for an additional sixty years and were ultimately able to secure British recognition of their equality with other Jamaicans. This group maintains a presence on the island of Jamaica today.

The Origins of Voodoo

The blending of the Taino and the Africans also led to the development of a new religion in the Greater Antilles. As African runaway slaves mixed with the surviving Taino, the religious traits of both groups merged into a spiritual practice called voodoo. Voodoo would eventually become one of the predominant religions of Haiti and other parts of the Caribbean.

In the dialects of western Africa, the word *voodoo* means "spirit." The voodoo spirits are called *loas* and, according to voodoo practitioners, live in trees. *Loas* are ancestral spirits which are similar to the gods and goddesses of Greek and Roman mythology in that they represent parts of nature.

The *loas* are also similar to the Taino *zemis* who were believed to control the weather and other aspects of life. Whereas the *zemis* acted as intermediaries between shamans and the primary god in Taino society, the *loas* themselves are thought to be powerful. "The loa," writes journalist Wade Davis, who spent time in Haiti studying this religion, "are powerful and if offended can do great harm, but they are also predictable, and if properly served, will reward men and women with good fortune."[52]

In the Taino religion, shamans took hallucinogens to enter a trancelike state to communicate with the gods. In voodoo, singing and dancing during voodoo ceremonies often lead to similar trances. Voodoo priests called *houcans* and priestesses called *mambos* can, practitioners believe, communicate with the *loas* during these trances. The dancing is all done to the sound of drums, rattles, and bamboo pipes.

Although North Americans and Europeans often think of voodoo in terms of curses and spells and animal sacrifices, Davis sees much more: "It is not a black magic cult; it is a system of profound religious beliefs concerning the relationship among men, nature, and the supernatural forces of the universe. [It] not only embodies a set of spiritual concepts, it prescribes a way of life, a philosophy, and code of ethics that regulate social behavior."[53]

Taino religion and spirituality governed every aspect of their life. Similarly, those who practice voodoo incorporate its concepts and rituals into their daily routines. In the twenty-first century, voodoo, or vodun as it is sometimes called, is primarily a religion of the poor.

The Black Carib

African slaves also interacted with the Carib on their island strongholds in the Lesser Antilles. The Carib fathered thousands of children with African runaway slave women. This mixture was the beginning of a group later known as the Black Carib.

The islands of Saint Vincent and Dominica in the Lesser Antilles became two Black Carib strongholds. Runaway slaves

The Carib of Saint Vincent

Much of the present-day population of the island of Saint Vincent has a mixture of African and Carib blood. Generally known as the Black Carib, these descendants of the original Carib exist on the windward coast of Saint Vincent. Most live in poverty.

Many of the houses on the island of Saint Vincent are made of boards with galvanized or thatched roofs. A wood-burning fireplace within the main house provides for warmth and cooking. Only a very few Carib families possess kerosene or wood stoves. Unemployment in the village on Saint Vincent is extremely high. Those children who do attend school have a high absentee rate and drop out of school by the end of the sixth grade. Many Carib children stay home year-round to help their parents pick and pack bananas to support their families.

The Carib of Saint Vincent are, however, important to that island's economy since they contribute arrowroot and bananas to the export market. They also practice subsistence farming. The Carib make up about 2 percent of the island's population. Many of them have adopted western ways in their food, dress, and religion.

Many of the Black Carib of Saint Vincent live in thatched huts like the one pictured here.

streamed there from neighboring islands until the population of the Black Carib numbered in the thousands. "Their tiny nation [on Dominica], an amalgam of Afro-Carib half-breeds with runaways from plantation slavery and castaways from wrecked slave ships," writes journalist Peter T. Muilenburg, "was a beacon of liberty in a sea of slavery for nearly 300 years."[54]

As time passed, the number of Africans began to exceed the number of pure Carib. Despite the dwindling Amerindian numbers, the Black Caribs, however, retained a great deal of Carib culture. They called themselves Carib and spoke the Carib language. They even flattened their foreheads as the Carib had done for generations. The Black Carib also buried their dead sitting up in the tradition of the Amerindians. And, like the Carib, they were a democratic society without rank or class distinction.

The Carib Choose to Fight

Unlike their Taino neighbors to the north who had initially treated the explorers with friendship, the Carib, from the beginning, greeted the European explorers and settlers with suspicion, and when threatened, fought back. "For 150 years after Columbus," writes Peter T. Muilenburg, "the Caribs raided Spanish towns and plantations in the eastern Caribbean, then terrorized the English, Dutch, and French settlements."[55] This resistance continued throughout the seventeenth and most of the eighteenth century.

The Carib had always had the reputation of being the fiercest and most warlike tribe in the Caribbean. With astonishing success, they were able to prevent the settlement of several islands in the Lesser Antilles group for several hundred years after the Taino had succumbed. In many cases the warriors were willing to fight to the death or launch suicidal last stands in order to fight for the freedom of their people.

Irvince Auguiste, former chief of the Carib community on the island of Dominica, spoke of those days with *National Geographic* journalist Robert Booth. Au-

guiste stated: "Columbus and those who followed were looking for gold. The Caribs had gold, which they traded for glass beads. When [my ancestors] realized they were being fooled, they started to retaliate. The Europeans tried to enslave them. Captured Caribs killed themselves by the hundreds, rather than submit. The Carib people continued to fight."[56]

Believing that their gods had deserted them, many of the Carib villagers opted for suicide rather than enslavement. In 1651, for instance, several dozen Carib on the island of Grenada leaped to their death at Sauters Cliff rather than surrender to the French. This cliff is known today as Carib Leap.

Rebellion on Trinidad

The Carib also gave the Caribbean its first major Amerindian rebellion in 1699. Called the Arena Uprising, the battle was led by a Carib warrior named Bustamante.

A new Catholic church was being built on the island of Trinidad. Two Carib laborers were working under the supervision of a monk and a Spanish carpenter. The natives were new to the task and did not grasp the intricacies of European construction practices. Their clumsiness, however, was apparently perceived as being a deliberate effort to sabotage the project.

The carpenter and monk made harsh remarks to the Amerindians and threatened to punish them severely. In a fit of anger, one of the Carib workers lifted his shovel and knocked the monk to the ground. When the Spanish carpenter rushed to his aid, the other Amerindian knifed him. The two Carib rallied the remaining mission Indians, and under the leadership of Bustamante proceeded to kill several priests and burn the mission to the ground.

Two months later, the Spanish sent soldiers to punish the rebellious Amerindians, driving them to the sea where a battle took place at Cocal Beach. Many of the Carib—men, women, and children—drowned themselves rather than be captured or killed by the Spanish.

Other Caribs were captured and taken to the town of Saint Joseph where they were tortured and then put on trial. Sixty-one warriors were sentenced to death. While the majority of the condemned were shot, at least twenty Carib men were dragged through the city and then hanged. According to historians, "Their hands and heads were cut off, their bodies quartered, and the pieces spiked on the public road."[57]

The remaining Carib on the islands of Trinidad and Tobago were eventually transported to other islands. This was done to make way for the influx of French planters and their African slaves. Many of the Carib fled to the islands of Saint Vincent and Dominica where they joined up with the Black Carib.

Black Carib Resistance

The Black Carib were put to the test in 1719 when the French decided to invade the island of Saint Vincent in order to enslave the Amerindians and any Africans also living there. The Black Carib, however, learned of the French plans in ad-

vance and decided to set a trap. They were able to lure the French to a spot particularly suited for ambush and let off a devastating volley of arrows and musket fire. The ambush was extremely effective, causing the French to flee and not return to the island.

Towards the end of the eighteenth century, the English became interested in the island of Saint Vincent. Their interest was due primarily to the richness of that island's soil and its potential for use in planting sugarcane. More and more British colonists came to the island to try their hand at planting. In 1763 the English annexed the island and announced that the Black Carib would have to accept British sovereignty and agree to a series of restrictions and regulations. These laws included the construction of a network of roads and military posts through the Carib territory.

Intermittent fighting between the settlers and the Carib turned eventually into a full-scale war. A British force was finally able to subdue the Carib in 1773. In that year, the British assumed control of half the island of Saint Vincent; the Carib were allowed to live unmolested on the other half.

Two years later the Caribs, dissatisfied with British incursions into their territory, revolted and overran the island with French assistance. The British had little difficulty in suppressing the rebellion, deporting most of the remaining Carib to British Honduras (present-day Belize) in 1797. The victorious colonists confined the remaining Carib population of Saint Vincent

Trinidad and Tobago

Trinidad has the distinction of being the first Caribbean island settled by both the Arawak and Carib Amerindians. Eventually, the Carib, a more warlike people, were able to kill off the Arawak and claim the island for their own.

Trinidad, along with Tobago, is the southernmost of the Caribbean islands, lying only a few miles off the coast of Venezuela. The two islands are part of the island chain known as the Windward Islands, a group that also contains the islands of Grenada, Dominica, and others.

The first Spanish settlement occurred on the island of Trinidad in 1592. That it took one hundred years after Columbus landed in the Caribbean for the island to be colonized was due entirely to the island's dense rainforests and the warlike Carib Indians. Both factors made settlement difficult. In the late sixteenth century, missionaries arrived and established missions to Christianize the Amerindians.

Originally settled by the Spanish, Trinidad and Tobago ultimately became French territory before being turned over to the English in 1803. The process toward independence for the islands began in 1962, and not long thereafter Trinidad and Tobago became part of the British Commonwealth.

A tribe watches the 1902 eruption of Mount Pelée in awe. The eruption destroyed entire villages.

to a reservation near Mount Soufrière, a volcano at the northern end of the island. The volcano erupted in 1902, within days of an even greater explosion of Mount Pelée on the island of Martinique, following a series of earthquakes that struck the Caribbean. The death toll on Saint Vincent reached sixteen hundred people, many of them descendants of the Black Carib.

The Carib of Dominica

The rugged terrain and dense forests of Dominica were particularly well suited to the Carib style of warfare. The Carib, as a result, were well entrenched in their mountain stronghold on this island. According to historians, "*Wai'tukubuli* [Dominica] with its inaccessible mountains and forests . . . became the last Carib stronghold and retreat [in the Caribbean]; a base for attacking neighboring colonies and the site of reprisal massacres."[58]

Beginning in the late fifteenth century, ships from all the European nations began to arrive on Dominica to cut down timber and plant crops. For almost two hundred years, contact between the Carib and the

Europeans was limited to a little trading and an occasional skirmish.

Christianity was first introduced on the island of Dominica in 1642 and soon missionaries installed themselves throughout the area. They had little success in Christianizing the Carib.

At the same time, however, newspapers and official reports from the various European nations began making charges that the Carib were vicious cannibals. Most of these charges were gross exaggerations, probably based on reports of the occasional consumption of ancestor and enemy remains

The lush forests and jagged coastal cliffs of Dominica offered natural protection to the Carib, enabling them to resist colonization for almost two hundred years.

by the Amerindians. However, according to historian Kirkpatrick Sale these reports "provided the means of justifying the enslavement [of the Carib.] It [the myth of widespread cannibalism] permitted the denigration, and thus the conquest and exploitation, of people whose lands were seen as increasingly desirable in European eyes."[59]

The British Take Over Dominica

The Carib of Dominica fought fiercely to keep the Europeans away. For nearly two hundred years, no European nation was able to conquer them or gain a real foothold on their island. But the long years of fighting and the effects of various European diseases began to take their toll on the Carib. By the early eighteenth century, only a few hundred Amerindians survived.

It was Great Britain that finally managed to take control of the island of Dominica in 1763. The English promptly divided the island into parcels of land that were offered to any colonist willing to settle on the island and raise crops. Settlers came in increasing numbers to establish plantations.

The British left about two hundred acres of land for the Carib. Living in relative isolation, the Carib were seldom seen by the growing European and African populations. Now and then the Carib appeared at markets to sell their homemade baskets or fish. This was the only contact between the Amerindians and other cultures until the late nineteenth century.

In 1893 the few remaining Carib on Dominica sent a petition to the British government in which they pleaded for assistance. They wrote: "We don't have nothing to support us, no church, no school, no shop, no store. We are very far in the forest, no money, no dress. They call us wild savages. . . . It is not savages but poverty."[60] Ten years later the British created a Carib Territory on the northeast coast of the island. There, the Carib lived in relative isolation and poverty, struggling to survive, while receiving little assistance from the British government.

Colonialism

During the years of conflict between the Amerindians and Europeans, and despite the determined resistance of the Taino and the Carib along with their African allies, the European powers were able to maintain and eventually increase their presence in the Caribbean. During the seventeenth and eighteenth centuries, Great Britain, Spain, the Netherlands, France, and Denmark all competed for their share of the islands. As a result, many of the islands changed hands numerous times. The island of Saint Lucia, for example, changed hands fourteen times between the British and the French before the British finally dominated and got the island for good in 1803.

England was by far the most successful of the European countries in its effort to challenge Spanish domination of the Caribbean. England was able to gain a stronghold in the area primarily because the Spanish lost interest. The Spanish quickly became

Haitian Independence

By the late eighteenth century, France had wrested part of Hispaniola away from the Spanish and developed an expansive plantation system. Conditions on the plantations were inhumane, with frequent tortures and beatings of the African slaves.

Bloody rebellion broke out in the western part of Hispaniola in 1791. The revolt was led by former slave Toussaint-Louverture. Nearly five hundred thousand blacks and a few surviving Taino joined him in a fight against the French leadership on the island. The rebels were successful in freeing the slaves and setting up a new government.

In 1802 the French retaliated. Louverture was captured and eventually executed. French soldiers took control of the western part of the island but their success was short-lived. As the rebels gained in strength, the French were forced to withdraw and in 1804 a new nation emerged.

The western third of the island became the independent black nation of Haiti. Independence was declared on January 1, 1804, and General Jean-Jacques Dessalines became the first black president of the first black republic anywhere in the world.

A former slave, Toussaint-Louverture led the successful revolt against the French on Hispaniola.

more interested in South America and Central America where the vast and wealthy Inca, Maya, and Aztec lived.

The United States became a colonial power in the Caribbean following the Spanish-American War of 1898. It was at this time that the United States took control of the island of Puerto Rico. In 1917 America bought part of the Virgin Islands from the Danes. During the twentieth century the United States sent troops to a number of Caribbean islands, including Cuba, the Dominican Republic, Grenada, and Haiti.

The Effects of Colonization

The primary effect of the colonization of the Caribbean was the near extinction of the Amerindians who lived there. The natives were also the victims of enslavement, social dislocation, and epidemics of disease.

The enslavement of vast portions of the Amerindian population led to the destruction of their former way of life. "The Europeans," writes historian Franklin W. Knight,

> who invaded and conquered the Caribbean destroyed the internally cohesive world of the native people. Their simple lives were regimented by slavery and the demands of profit-oriented, commerce-minded Europeans. Above all, they were slowly inundated culturally . . . by the stream of new immigrants. . . . Their social and political organizations were restructured in the name of Christianity.[61]

Disease also played a large part in the conquest of the New World. The Amerindians who lived in the Caribbean had no immunity to fight the diseases the Europeans brought with them. As a result, smallpox, measles, diphtheria, typhoid, cholera, tuberculosis, and scarlet fever epidemics swept through the native populations. In 1527, for instance, a smallpox epidemic on the island of Puerto Rico killed nearly one-third of the Taino who lived there.

The concentrated populations of Amerindians that had lived on the islands of the Caribbean prior to the time of Columbus's first voyage declined rapidly as the result of all these factors. Overwork, brutality, and European diseases eliminated entire island populations. Despite the near decimation of their people, and contrary to the myths and reports of the time, small groups of Taino and Carib survived in small isolated locations throughout the Caribbean.

Chapter 6

The Amerindians in Today's Caribbean

For hundreds of years, historians, scholars, and government officials in the Caribbean and elsewhere stated unequivocally that the Amerindians of the Caribbean became extinct very shortly after the Spanish arrived. Amerindian extinction is, in fact, a myth. While the Lucayans failed to survive the harsh treatment of the Spanish, the Carib and the Taino did survive and, in the late twentieth century, begin to reclaim their heritage. As historian Paul Reddish states: "After centuries when native cultures have been denigrated and reviled, new groups are springing up across the Caribbean who are emphasizing their native ancestry."[62]

The Taino of Puerto Rico are today enjoying a resurgence of their ancient culture, while the Carib have long maintained their presence on the island of Dominica. The Carib are also making their voices heard on the islands of Trinidad and Saint Vincent. Throughout the Caribbean, Amerindian groups are speaking out about their history and their survival.

The Myth of Taino Extinction

"History books . . . still refer to the Taino/Arawak people as the first tribe to be decimated by colonialism," writes journalist Richard L. Vasquez.

> It would be more appropriate to say that this was the first tribe to be told they were extinct. . . . Because the government does not recognize them or because they haven't maintained a very public presence, we assume that their stories ended in our grade school textbooks saying they were conquered. While their governments and temples fell, the people remained and continued to influence our culture—and ancestry.[63]

Hundreds, if not thousands, of Spanish colonists married Taino women. It has been estimated, in fact, that nearly 40 percent of the Spanish men who visited the island of Hispaniola fathered children with Taino women and then returned to Spain without them. Despite the fact that the

Descendants of the Taino Amerindians, like the man pictured here, have retained many traditions of their ancestors.

Taino disappeared from the census records in the early 1500s as an ethnic group, Taino families were simply recategorized as peasants or Spanish citizens. In reality, the Taino and their ancestors continued to follow their ancient way of life in the mountainous interiors on the islands of Puerto Rico, Hispaniola, Jamaica, and Cuba.

On the island of Puerto Rico, for instance, the Tainos were classified as "Indian" until the beginning of the twentieth century. At that time, Governor do Toribiq Montes, faced with the difficulty of fixing ethnic origins, banded all the nonwhites together under the title of "free colored people."

The Taino of Puerto Rico

Descendants of the original Taino Amerindians still follow a traditional way of life on such islands as Cuba and the Dominican Republic, although the census records call them Cubans or Dominicans. This also seems to be the case in Puerto Rico where recent DNA studies show that many people who are classified as Puerto Ricans are in reality of Taino heritage.

The Taino, in the days before Columbus, called the island of Puerto Rico *Borinquén,* meaning "the land of the brave lord." Today, the ancestors of the original Taino people of that island are united together, calling themselves the Jatibonicu tribe. These "Great People of the Sacred High Waters" also go by the name of the Jíbaro mountain people. The tribe makes its home in the central mountains on the island of Puerto Rico.

According to Taino cacique Pedro Guanikeyu Torres in a 2002 interview with journalist Richard L. Vasquez, "Our Taino way of life and its culture remains alive as long as we Tainos continue to live it and to share it with others."[64]

It was in the late 1960s that members of the Taino tribe organized and affirmed their presence in Puerto Rico. Today the Taino are working to defend their rights as an indigenous people. "We seek to obtain the full Federal and State recognition and mutual respect between our common governments in Puerto Rico and the United States,"[65] Torres told Vasquez.

This desire for recognition was reflected in a letter to the Puerto Rican people written by the Taino tribe of Jatibonicu. "We are the surviving descendants of the original indigenous people of the island of Boriken [*Borinquén* or Puerto Rico]. . . . Please help us in our struggle to preserve our past tribal traditions and customs of our Taino aboriginal way of life."[66] This letter, written in November 1970, was sent to the Puerto Rican people as a plea for the official recognition of the Jatibonicu as an indigenous group.

Gaining Independence

Haiti was the first Caribbean island to gain independence from its colonial ruler. This occurred after the rebellion of 1804. In 1865 the remaining part of Hispaniola—the Dominican Republic—proclaimed its own independence from Spain, followed by Cuba in 1898. No other changes occurred until after World War II.

Most of the remaining Caribbean societies were decolonized after World War II, either receiving full independence or becoming incorporated into the "mother" country. Jamaica, Trinidad, and Tobago are among those who became members of the British Commonwealth, the independent nations who were once colonies of the British Empire.

Today there are three republics in the Caribbean—Cuba, Haiti, and the Dominican Republic. The governments on Hispaniola are democracies, although Haiti is still controlled by the army. Cuba is a Communist nation, since 1959 led by one man, Fidel Castro.

Puerto Rico

The last island nation to be settled by the Amerindians, Puerto Rico was called *Borinquén* or "the land of the brave lord" by the original Taino inhabitants. When Christopher Columbus arrived on the island, he christened it *La Isla del Encanto,* meaning the "Island of Enchantment." The name was later changed to *Puerto Rico,* a Spanish phrase for "rich port."

Just as Puerto Rico was gaining some self-sufficiency in the eighteenth and nineteenth centuries, the Spanish were coincidentally losing their position as a world power. Spain's troubles began in the eighteenth century when that nation found itself in a contest with Great Britain for land and power in the Caribbean and North America. Spain lost many of the colonies to the British but was able to maintain control of both Cuba and Puerto Rico.

After the Spanish-American War of 1898, however, Cuba and Puerto Rico came under the protection of the United States which wanted to be able to use both islands for the defense of the Caribbean and the newly built Panama Canal.

Today Puerto Rico is a self-governing unit that is, by consent of the people, politically and economically linked to the United States. Puerto Ricans are citizens of the United States although they pay no federal taxes and are not allowed to vote in American presidential elections.

Puerto Rico today has one of the most diversified manufacturing economies in the Caribbean, producing more goods than all the other islands combined. It is a very modern country where education is a high priority, resulting in a 90 percent literacy rate.

The Santa Rosa Amerindian Community of Trinidad

The Santa Rosa Amerindian Community is the only organized group of Carib Indians on the islands of Trinidad and Tobago. Once a stronghold for the Carib, Trinidad today boasts a community of around four hundred Carib. Located in the town of Arema, Trinidad, the community includes a council of elders who are charged with maintaining Carib traditional history and knowledge.

The Santa Rosa Carib Community is the last remaining organized group of people on Trinidad who identify with and attempt to preserve their Amerindian way of life. Santa Rosa is also a leading member of the Caribbean Organization for Indigenous People.

Plans are underway in this new millennium for the establishment of an Amerindian Heritage Complex near Arema on the island of Trinidad. Adjoining the proposed housing complex will be a 375-acre forest reserve where the Santa Rosa Caribs will plant maize, cassava, and different fruits much as the early Amerindians did. It is hoped that these plans will provide some sorely needed jobs and income for the Carib community.

The Carib Community on Dominica

The small island of Dominica is the home of around three thousand Carib Indians, all of whom are descendants of the original inhabitants of the island. Today they live in the Carib Territory, an area comprising thirty thousand acres of land. In 1903 the British government proclaimed this area to be the exclusive domain of the Amerindians.

The Carib Territory is the home of the Kalinago tribe of Carib who once ruled much of the eastern Caribbean. Their land is located on the northeast coast of the island, the site of the original Carib Territory, where the Carib live in eight separate villages and keep pretty much to themselves.

In 1952 a Carib Council was created on the island of Dominica as part of a local government system that was instituted across the entire island. Elections are now held every five years within the Carib community to select a chairman who is designated their

The self-governing Carib Territory on Dominica is home to many descendants of the original Carib Amerindians, such as those pictured here.

chief. The Carib also elect a parliamentary representative to sit in the Dominica House of Assembly. This representative serves a five-year term and has more actual power than the chairman, although the two do make an effort to work together on behalf of their people.

Visually there is little to differentiate the Carib Territory from any other part of rural Dominica. According to local historians:

The same small farms of mixed crops dominated by bananas and coconuts are clustered around the roadsides and surrounding hills. The same houses, some of concrete, some of wood, surrounded by tidy flower gardens face onto the road. . . . Increasingly you'll see the family pick-up truck parked nearby and television aerials sprouting from bamboo poles.[67]

Many of the Carib homes, however, are up on stilts in order to shelter the drying crops of cocoa and coffee and the reeds that are used for weaving baskets.

Problems Facing the Amerindians

The Taino and Carib face many of the same problems that affect the majority of people living in the Caribbean today. These problems include racism, poverty, unemployment, poor health care, and inadequate schooling and housing.

The Amerindians, like thousands of other ethnic groups in the Caribbean, live in poverty and survive on subsistence

---

Dominica

Lacking the wide sandy beaches that attract tourists to other Caribbean islands, Dominica has instead the largest area of tropical forest in the entire region, covering over 40 percent of the land. Instead of the large influx of vacationers that other islands have, Dominica has remained largely unspoiled. The small island (twenty-nine miles long and thirteen miles wide) is also the Caribbean's most mountainous island, and the wettest. Despite recent economic upswings, Dominica remains one of the poorest islands in the Caribbean.

Dominica was granted full independence from Great Britain on November 3, 1978, but it chose to remain a part of the British Commonwealth. Unlike most of the other Caribbean islands, Dominica has changed little in the last two hundred years. It remains largely unsettled.

The island also contains the largest settlement of Carib found anywhere in the Caribbean. The Amerindians continue to reside on land that was granted them in 1903 by the British government.

Like many Caribbean families, this woman and her child live in a run-down home. Poverty and homelessness afflict much of the Caribbean population.

farming. The land is generally treated like a big family or community farm with all of the harvests going to feed the community. There is seldom enough food to provide a balanced diet. As a result, malnutrition has become a significant problem for many Caribbean Amerindians.

Many families in the Caribbean live in run-down housing without electricity, waste disposal, or indoor plumbing. Electricity and telephone service, for instance, did not make an appearance in the Carib Territory on Dominica until well into the 1980s. Even in the twenty-first century, there are still homes in the Carib Territory without indoor plumbing.

Thousands of Caribbean residents still live in shacks made of wood and sheets of corrugated iron or tin. Many of the older homes on the islands are small wooden buildings raised above the ground on stilts. Cities are generally overcrowded. In the Dominican Republic, for instance, as the cities fill up with rural families looking for work, the streets fill up with makeshift shelters constructed of boxes or anything else that is available. Many Caribbean cities have sizable homeless populations.

Some Amerindians own their own land but many still work on banana and sugarcane plantations. The majority of families have no cars so that in many rural areas the main method of transportation is by foot or on donkeys.

Poverty in a Tropical Paradise

The Carib who live on the island of Dominica make very little money. They make and sell baskets and dugout canoes but there is little demand for most of what they produce. The Carib also sell fruit and vegetables at roadside stands and work on banana farms. Most of the Carib are now farmers, not fishermen as their ancestors were. "It is a sad irony that this [former] group of seafarers, after whom the waters of the Carib have been named," write historians, "should end up in a corner of the island where access to the sea is almost impossible."[68]

Poverty is particularly hard for the Amerindian children in the Caribbean. Carib children, for instance, have few bought toys. Rather, they use plant parts to make toys much as their ancestors once did. Coconut leaves can be made into windmills while plant stalks are often used to make dolls.

Education and Health Care

Education is compulsory on most of the Caribbean islands for children up to the

Children study at a Caribbean school. Although education is free and compulsory, rural children frequently miss school in order to help their families in the fields.

Cuba

The largest island in the Caribbean, Cuba also contains the largest population today, numbering around 10 million. Originally occupied by the Taino, its nineteenth-century population of descendants of Spanish colonists and runaway slaves gained independence following the Spanish-American War in 1898.

On January 1, 1959, Fidel Castro and an army of over eight hundred men overthrew the oppressive and abusive regime of dictator Fulgencio Batista. Castro quickly took control of the island and aligned himself with the Soviet Union, at the time a monolithic Communist nation.

The Cuban government today provides free and equal education for all, regardless of sex or race. The educational system focuses on teaching many practical and technical skills that will enable the students to quickly find work following graduation. Education begins in day care centers, where children receive free meals and are taught simple skills to prepare them for further education. Even university education is free, but only students who have good high school grades and pass stringent examinations are accepted.

Health care services are also free and are provided by a network of neighborhood family doctors, who must live on the same street they work. It is not unusual for Cuban doctors to make house calls. In fact, people who have not had a physical or medical checkup for more than six months can expect a visit from the nearest doctor.

Anthropologists believe that a few Taino live on Cuba today, despite brutal efforts to enslave and kill their ancestors. The Communist regime, however, has not permitted scholars and DNA testers to investigate the matter.

age of eleven or twelve. Education on most of the islands is also free. In many of the poorer areas, schools are often simple wooden huts where one teacher offers instruction to children of all ages.

Amerindian and other Caribbean children who live in rural areas generally have poor school records due to their frequent absences. Many families need their children to help work in the fields and feel that education is but a secondary concern.

Most, if not all, of the children in the Carib Territory of Dominica attend the Sinalo Primary School. In addition to their studies, the students take care of the land around the school. They often play rounders, a British ball game in which the batter hits a pitched ball and runs around the bases. Instead of store-bought bats, the children often play with the branches of coconut trees.

Ill health is an ongoing problem for many people of the Caribbean. The problems range from malnutrition to AIDS. These diseases are especially prevalent on the island of Haiti and in many rural areas on the other islands. Many people, including the Taino and Carib, still rely on traditional folk medicine for the treatment of diseases that in the developed world are treated with antibiotics and other modern drugs.

A United States $28 million health and population project for the Caribbean is currently being funded by the World Bank. This project intends to extend health services to the Haitian poor. Its goal is to reduce tuberculosis by 50 percent and also set up an AIDS program in Hispaniola where those two diseases are endemic.

Overpopulation and Unemployment

Most of the islands of the Caribbean are overpopulated. Where land is limited, as it is in the Caribbean, any population increase can be a threat to the environment and the economy. Increased pollution due

Many Taino farmers, like the one pictured here, have taken low-paying jobs in the cities to supplement their meager incomes.

to the rapid expansion of industry in the islands in recent years is adding to the problem. Fresh water is also in very short supply on many of the islands. In fact, for many residents of the Caribbean, cisterns and other receptacles that collect rain are the only source of drinking water.

The last thirty years of the twentieth century saw the growth of a number of significant industries in the Caribbean. Many of the islands are now building factories that produce electrical goods, textiles, and clothing. Plastics, sports equipment, and medicine are also being produced in great quantities. With the advent of these industries, more jobs have become available.

The Amerindians of the Caribbean, however, are usually ill prepared to obtain jobs in these growing industries. Lacking the necessary skills to work in factories and often not having had enough education to be able to read simple instructions, hundreds of the Taino and Carib remain unemployed.

The Taino have had a little better success than their Carib neighbors at adapting to the newly industrialized status of Puerto Rico. In the late twentieth century, many of the Taino left the mountains and began to accept low-paying jobs as a supplement to their farming, fishing, and hunting. The Carib, on the other hand, continue to eke out their livings through subsistence farming and the selling of many of their traditional wares.

The Effect of Tourism

Tourism is the single most important source of income on most of the Caribbean islands today. The Caribbean has long been an ideal vacation spot because of its beautiful beaches, its phenomenal scenery, and its first-class hotels. The islands, in recent years, have also become a favorite destination for cruise ships.

The tourist industry has provided a large number of jobs for the islanders. Tourism has also led to jobs in construction, catering, and transportation. In the Bahamas, for instance, the tourist industry employs over two-thirds of the total workforce. Many of the jobs, however, pay very little and offer few chances for advancement.

Even so, several of the islands, most notably Dominica, are now attempting to take advantage of their indigenous history to attract tourists. In the last twenty years there has been widespread interest in the re-creation of an original Carib village on the island of Dominica. This interest has been shared by the Carib people and by the government of that island. Cultural villages of this type have been, in the last thirty years, springing up in areas of the Pacific and in North America with great success.

Journalist Jonathan B. Tourtellot, on a 2002 trip to Dominica, visited the Carib Territory. He reports that the Carib have long wanted to create an historically accurate fifteenth-century Carib village for the purpose of educating visitors about their history. According to Tourtellot, "Somehow this admirable project ended up in the hands—not of the Indians, not of anthropologists—but of government engineers."[69]

The result was a supposedly authentic village that was hurricane-proof. The problem,

Beautiful beaches like that of Montego Bay attract thousands of tourists to the islands of the Caribbean. Tourism has created many jobs for residents.

unfortunately, was that in order to make the village totally hurricane-proof, the builders used concrete, a material not available six hundred years ago. The project was a fiasco.

The Carib decided to take matters into their own hands. Just up the road from the government's project lies Karina Village, a Carib-owned and Carib-operated facility. Karina Village showcases authentic Carib culture, including dancing, crafts, and music. The village is made from the same materials used by the Carib ancestors centuries ago, and has thus far proven to be hurricane-proof.

Needs of the Amerindians Today

White elitism, a by-product of the colonial plantation system, is hampering the efforts of the Taino and Carib to improve their standard of living and overcome the problems they face today. Island governments tend to be run predominantly by white people, who are better educated and far better off economically than the majority populations of blacks, Amerindians, and other ethnic groups. As a result, there is a wide discrepancy in the lifestyles of the two classes. There is also evidence of prejudice and discrimination in the availability of jobs, education, housing, and many other facets of day-to-day life. This racism has often made it difficult for the Carib and the Taino to advance economically or socially.

Irvince Auguiste was the chief of the Carib Community on the island of Dominica when *National Geographic* journalist Robert Booth visited there in the late 1980s. Auguiste, at the time, lived with his wife and four children in a two-room house with no running water. Auguiste spoke of the needs of the Carib Community:

> Descendants of the African slaves are today doctors and lawyers. We need Carib doctors and lawyers, and we need our own secondary schools if our children are to remain Carib. Most of all, we need our own financial institutions so Carib people can use their land, which is held in common, as collateral for loans. We could then begin to build an economic base.[70]

Adding to the already significant problems facing them today, the Carib and Taino also must contend with the rapid loss of their cultural identity. It is their traditional ways of life, their language, and their customs that have made the Amerindians unique. "Intermarriage, the virtual disappearance of the . . . language," according to historians, along with "the harsh economics of small island life, and the incursions of the global village (from drugs to crime to dancehalls to brand-name clothes) have all taken their toll on [Amerindian] identity."[71]

"There are laws to preserve the wildlife of Dominica," said Auguiste. "Surely the native people of Dominica should be preserved."[72]

These statements are true of the Taino as well.

Hope for the Future

Despite the myths of extinction from the past and the problems of today, the Carib and Taino are alive and well in the Caribbean. Amerindian elders continue to pass on ancient myths through storytelling, while others teach traditional skills in an effort to keep dances, crafts, legends, beliefs, and ways of life alive.

The Taino

Taino cacique Pedro Guanikeyu Torres, in an interview with Richard L. Vasquez, spoke of the goals of the Taino in the twenty-first century. He stated: "We are not about money, we are about correcting history and honoring of our past Taino ancestors. We with all fairness look to . . . what was taken from us by the colonials back in 1493 and to reestablish a sovereign Taino Tribal nation and our own sovereign homeland."[73]

To achieve those aims, the Taino formed the United Confederation of Taino People (UCTP) in 1998. This confederation is an international group of Caribbean indigenous people that is, according to the organization's charter, "dedicated to the promotion and protection of the cultural heritage and spiritual traditions of their aboriginal ancestors."[74]

The Confederation gives the Taino a way to present a unified voice in their efforts to address the multiplicity of problems that face the Caribbean Amerindians in the modern world. These issues include the promotion of indigenous cultures and people, the protection of the environment and wildlife, the correction of historical myths and misconceptions, and the preservation and management of various sacred sites throughout the Caribbean.

The Confederation currently has regional representatives in Puerto Rico, the Dominican Republic, and the United States. In an effort to gather statistical information that will further document the survival of their people, the Taino Confederation has also recently established a population census registry.

The Carib

The Carib have also become politically active in an attempt to establish their status as an indigenous people. In March 2002 representatives from the Carib Territory of Dominica traveled to Quebec to attend an important meeting of thousands of indigenous people from all over the world. At the Eagle and Condor Indigenous Action Summit, Carib chief Joseph Garnet, representing his people, signed an agreement between the Carib Council and an international umbrella group called the First Nations Business Association.

This was a momentous gathering, for it was an opportunity for the Carib people to announce to the world that they had survived and were assuming a role in the worldwide community of indigenous people. One result of the meeting was the creation of an Aboriginal Communication Network that would enable the Carib to maintain contact with other indigenous groups around the world. A business fund was set up to assist the Carib Territory to develop its resources and to address the key issues of poverty and unemployment on their reservation.

Links with the Past

The Carib and Taino, while attempting to improve their ways of life in the modern world, are also intent on preserving their links with the past. For the Carib, one of the strongest links is the baskets the Carib sell in little craft shops all along the road in Carib Territory. Such a basket is one of the few truly authentic indigenous souvenirs that a tourist can obtain from the region. The brown, white, and black designs have been handed down through the generations. Their waterproof construction is a remnant from the days when food and goods had to be kept dry during the rainy season and on long canoe voyages.

Caribbean music and dance, while having a special character of their own, also have their roots in many different ethnic

A Taino girl poses with her father. Taino and Carib elders pass their peoples' history and traditions on to younger generations.

A carnival dancer shows off her elaborate costume. Yearly carnivals are the modern equivalents of the Taino areytos, *preserving an ancient tradition of music and dance.*

traditions. Music and dance, from their origins with the Taino and Carib Indians, have always played a central role in the lives of the people who live in the Caribbean. The Amerindians and those who followed used music and dance as a way of showing pride in their traditional ways of life.

Influenced by the original Amerindians, the Africans, Europeans, and others, Caribbean music ranges from the lively and carefully written songs of the calypso singers of Trinidad to the reggae music of Jamaica. Caribbean music is now famous all over the world and in recent years has developed into an important industry.

The Taino *areytos* of the past have today been replaced with the carnival celebrations that are held on most of the islands of the Caribbean. The idea of an annual festival to celebrate the past and welcome the beginning of a new year was a common practice among the Amerindians. Carnivals today are also times for celebration and come complete with music, dancing, and fantastic costumes.

Today's music makes wide use of the maracas and drums used by the Amerindians. The sound of the drum, in particular, is very important to modern Caribbean musical styles. The most famous drums of recent history are the so-called steel drums made from abandoned oil drums. The origin of this type of drum dates back to the 1930s when musicians in Trinidad used oil drums as instruments because they could not afford anything else.

Calypso music, in particular, is reminiscent of the kind of music sung at *areytos*. Calypso singers often tell stories with their singing, just as the indigenous people did. The most popular songs are those that make people laugh. These songs might be funny stories about important people or silly stories about animals. All celebrate the heritage of the Caribbean.

A Success Story

Jacob Frederick is one of the thousands of Carib who today live on the island of Dominica. An artist and a leader, Frederick has, according to local historians, "risen beyond the daily struggle for survival and [has attempted] to instill a sense of pride in Carib identity among the young people of the [Carib] Territory and an awareness of the Carib presence and culture throughout the region."[75]

Now in his forties, Frederick is a self-taught artist whose lifework is documenting important events in Carib history. He is also attempting to preserve Carib myths, legends, and aspects of the his people's culture.

Frederick is responsible for conceiving the historic 1997 Carib Canoe Project. On this voyage of rediscovery, Frederick and his crew constructed an authentic Carib dugout canoe out of a single gommier tree just as his ancestors once did. He and his group sailed from the island of Dominica to the Carib ancestral grounds in South America—the original voyage of migration in reverse.

Frederick is now relearning the Carib traditional method of making hammocks. He is also a well-known artist, painter, and carver. His most impressive work to date is a complex wood carving called *Legends*. This piece, according to the artist, celebrates local Carib myths and legends and features a great snake at the base, shown emerging from the sea.

Jacob Frederick is but one example of the growing group of Carib and Taino Amerindians who are making their mark on Caribbean society in the twenty-first century.

Hope for the Future

Increasingly the indigenous people of the Caribbean are emphasizing the special qualities of their culture. They are making efforts to ensure that in a rapidly changing world their traditional language, folk tales, and way of life are not lost.

Nancy Jawaru Lion-Storm had been told as a child of her Taino heritage. She asserts,

I always thought of myself as Puerto Rican Taino. And throughout my whole life, when I mentioned to other Puerto Ricans that I was part Taino, they replied that I couldn't be. They said the Taino are extinct. . . . This same thing happened when I was in college, where the professors told me that I couldn't possibly be Taino. But I knew they were wrong.[76]

Indeed they were wrong. Their error was clearly demonstrated in a recent celebration. On November 21, 1998, men, women and children in traditional indigenous clothing came together to sing, dance, feast, and pray as Taino—the same people supposedly eradicated by the Spanish.

Like their neighbors the Carib, the Taino people are proud to be part of an ancient culture that is alive and growing.

Notes

Introduction: Who Are the Indigenous People of the Caribbean?

1. *El Museo,* "The Taino World," August 13, 2002. www.elmuseo.org.
2. Louise B. Young, *Islands.* New York: W.H. Freeman and Company, 1999, p. 183.

Chapter One: Adapting to Life in the Caribbean

3. Quoted in Alvin M. Josephy Jr., *America in 1492.* New York: Alfred A. Knopf, 1992, p. 147.
4. Josephy, *America in 1492*, p. 149.
5. Quoted in Robert Siegel and Sally Watt, "Taino Indians," *All Things Considered*, National Public Radio, October 12, 1998.
6. Kirkpatrick Sale, *The Conquest of Paradise.* New York: Alfred A. Knopf, 1990, p. 99.
7. *Pre-Columbian Hispaniola,* "Arawak-Taino Indians," August 13, 2002. www.hartford-hwp.com.
8. Quoted in Paul Reddish, *Spirits of the Jaguar.* London: BBC Books, 1996, p. 193.
9. Reddish, *Spirits of the Jaguar,* p. 153.
10. Margaret Morris, "The Land and the People," *Discover Jamaica.* www.discoverjamaica.com.

Chapter Two: Amerindian Society and Culture

11. Reddish, *Spirits of the Jaguar*, p. 148.
12. Michael D. Lemonick, "Archaeology: Before Columbus Destroyed." *Time,* October 19, 1998.
13. Josephy, *America in 1492,* p. 149.
14. Franklin W. Knight, "Caribbean Commonwealth," *Countries of the World*, January 1, 1991.
15. Carleton Mitchell, *Isles of the Caribees.* Washington, DC: National Geographic Books, 1968, p. 93.
16. Mitchell, *Isles of the Caribees*, p. 93.
17. Peter T. Muilenburg, "Black Carib Bastion of Freedom," *Americas 51*, May 1, 1999.
18. Manuel Lucena Salmoral, *America 1492: Portrait of a Continent Five Hundred Years Ago.* New York: Facts On File, 1990, p. 117.
19. Morris, "The Land and the People."
20. *Government of the Jatibonicu Taino People,* "Taino Culture," August 13, 2002. www.taino-tribe.org.
21. *El Museo,* "The Taino World."
22. *El Museo,* "The Taino World."
23. *El Museo,* "The Taino World."

Chapter Three: Amerindian Spirituality and Religion

24. Reddish, *Spirits of the Jaguar,* p. 163.

25. Josephy, *America in 1492*, p. 152.

26. Salmoral, *America 1492*, p. 218.

27. *El Museo*, "The Taino World."

28. *El Museo*, "The Taino World."

29. Reddish, *Spirits of the Jaguar*, p. 163.

30. Knight, "Caribbean Commonwealth."

31. Quoted in Robert Booth, "Dominica," *National Geographic*, June 1990, p. 108.

32. Reddish, *Spirits of the Jaguar*, p. 160.

33. Josephy, *America in 1492*, p. 154.

Chapter Four: The Discovery of the New World

34. Reddish, *Spirits of the Jaguar*, p. 12.

35. Knight, "Caribbean Commonwealth."

36. Knight, "Caribbean Commonwealth."

37. Sale, *The Conquest of Paradise*, p. 14.

38. Young, *Islands*, p. 184.

39. Quoted in Sale, *The Conquest of Paradise*, p. 100.

40. Quoted in Young, *Islands*, p. 184.

41. Quoted in Sale, *The Conquest of Paradise*, p. 96.

42. Quoted in Sale, *The Conquest of Paradise*, p. 139.

43. Sale, *The Conquest of Paradise*, p. 143.

44. Young, *Islands*, p. 184.

45. Quoted in Kim Johnson, "Taino," *Race and History*, August 13, 2002. www.raceandhistory.com.

46. Quoted in Sale, *The Conquest of Paradise*, p. 157.

47. Quoted in Reddish, *Spirits of the Jaguar*, p. 198.

48. Sale, *The Conquest of Paradise*, p. 154.

49. Reddish, *Spirits of the Jaguar*, p. 164.

50. Quoted in Johnson, "Taino."

51. Sale, *The Conquest of Paradise*, p. 112.

Chapter Five: The Growth of Colonial Empires

52. Wade Davis, *Shadows of the Sun,* Washington, DC: Island Press, 1998, p. 57.

53. Davis, *Shadows of the Sun,* p. 54.

54. Muilenburg, "Black Carib Bastion of Freedom."

55. Muilenburg, "Black Carib Bastion of Freedom."

56. Quoted Booth, "Dominica," p. 108.

57. *Amerindian Trail,* "An Indian Rebellion in Trinidad, 1699," August 13, 2002. www.amerindiantrail.com

58. *Indigenous Dominica—The Caribs*, "Caribs Yesterday and Today," August 13, 2002. www.geocities.com.

59. Sale, *The Conquest of Paradise*, p. 135.

60. *Indigenous Dominica—The Caribs*, "Caribs Yesterday and Today."

61. Knight, "Caribbean Commonwealth."

Chapter Six: The Amerindians in Today's Caribbean

62. Reddish, *Spirits of the Jaguar*, p. 209.

63. Richard L. Vasquez, "The Taino Survival," *Las Culturas*, August 13, 2002. www.lasculturas.com.

64. Quoted in Vasquez, "The Taino Survival."

65. Quoted in Vasquez, "The Taino Survival."

66. Government of the Jatibonicu Taino People, "Taino Culture," August 13, 2002. www.taino-tribe.com.

67. *Indigenous Dominica—The Caribs*, "Caribs Yesterday and Today."
68. *Indigenous Dominica—The Caribs,* "Caribs Yesterday and Today."
69. Jonathan B. Tourtellot, "Unspoiled in Spite of Itself," *National Geographic Traveler*, November/December 2002.
70. Quoted in Booth, "Dominica."
71. *Indigenous Dominica—The Caribs*, "Caribs Yesterday and Today."
72. Quoted in Booth, "Dominica."

Epilogue: Hope for the Future
73. Quoted in Vasquez, "The Taino Survival."
74. The United Confederation of Taino People, "UCTP General Information." www.uctp.org.
75. *Indigenous Dominica—The Caribs,* "Caribs Yesterday and Today."
76. Quoted in *Hispanic*, "Nacion Taina Recovered and Restored," February 28, 1999.

For Further Reading

Robert Barlas, *Bahamas*. New York: Marshall Cavendish, 2000. This book offers a comprehensive look at the islands of the Bahamas, including the history and people of the islands.

Paul Dash, *Traditions from the Caribbean*. Austin, TX: Raintree, Steck-Vaughn, 1999. This excellent book looks at the various cultural traditions of the Caribbean islands and where they originated.

Lucile Davis, *Puerto Rico*. New York: Childrens Press, 2000. This book gives an overall look at Puerto Rico, its history, and its people.

Allison Hodge, *The West Indies*. Austin, TX: Raintree, Steck-Vaughn, 1998. An overall look at the region of the Caribbean and its people.

Antony Mason, *The Caribbean: People and Places*. Englewood Cliffs, NJ: Silver Burdett, 1989. An overall look at the islands: history, people, and the way of life.

T.W. Mayer, *The Caribbean and Its People*. New York: Thomson Learning, 1995. An overall look at the islands, the people who lived there in the past, and those who live there today.

Lura Rogers and Barbara Radcliffe, *The Dominican Republic*. New York: Childrens Press, 1999. An overall look at the Dominican Republic, its history, and its people.

Frank Staub, *Children of Dominica*. Minneapolis: Carolrhoda Books, 1999. This book offers a great account of the Carib Indians who still live on the island of Dominica today.

Cas Walker, *Focus on the Caribbean*. London: Evans Brothers, 1988. An overall look at the Caribbean, including a section devoted to the indigenous people who lived there.

Works Consulted

Books

Wade Davis, *Shadows of the Sun.* Washington, DC: Island Press, 1998. This book is a compilation of essays written by the author on his travels to many lands. There is an excellent chapter on Haiti and the practice of voodoo.

Alvin M. Josephy Jr., *America in 1492.* New York: Alfred A. Knopf, 1992. An excellent book about the world of the Indian people throughout the Americas before the arrival of Christopher Columbus.

Lands and People of North America. Danbury, CT: Grolier Educational, 1999. This book contains good sections on the Bahamas and other islands of the Caribbean, including excellent coverage of the Native Americans who lived there.

Helen Chapin Metz, *Dominican Republic and Haiti: Country Studies.* Washington, DC: Federal Research Division, Library of Congress, 2001. A comprehensive look at these two Caribbean nations, including information about the original inhabitants.

Carleton Mitchell, *Isles of the Caribees.* Washington, DC: National Geographic Books, 1968. An excellent account of the author's travel throughout the Caribbean as he retraces the route taken by the Carib Indians. He also visits their enclave on the island of Dominica.

Paul Reddish, *Spirits of the Jaguar.* London: BBC Books, 1996. An excellent book in which the author describes the natural history of the Caribbean and South America, while also describing the ancient civilizations of both areas.

Kirkpatrick Sale, *The Conquest of Paradise.* New York: Alfred A. Knopf, 1990. An excellent book tracing Columbus's voyages to the New World and the impact these voyages had on the Indians who lived on the various Caribbean islands.

Manuel Lucena Salmoral, *America 1492: Portrait of a Continent Five Hundred Years Ago.* New York: Facts On File, 1990. An interesting look at the Amerindian world of 1492, including a good section about the Indians of the Caribbean.

Mike Tidwell, *In the Mountains of Heaven.* New York: Lyons Press, 2000. This book contains a number of essays written by this journalist, including one that tells of his adventures on a small island in the Bahamas.

Louise B. Young, *Islands.* New York: W.H. Freeman and Company, 1999. This naturalist focuses on several different island groups in a series of essays, including one on the Bahamas.

Periodicals

Robert Booth, "Dominica," *National Geographic,* June 1990.

Mary Jo Cosover, "St. Vincent and the Grenadines," *Countries of the World*, January 1, 1991.

Hispanic, "Nacion Taina Recovered and Restored," February 28, 1999.

Mark Holston, "Trails of Survival," *Americas* 47, March 13, 1995.

Franklin W. Knight, "Caribbean Commonwealth," *Countries of the World*, January 1, 1991.

Michael D. Lemonick, "Archaeology: Before Columbus Destroyed," *Time*, October 19, 1998.

Peter T. Muilenburg, "Black Carib Bastion of Freedom," *Americas* 51, May 1, 1999.

Eric P. Olsen, "Mountain Rebels," *The World and I*, February 1, 2000.

Karen Sturges-Vera, "Antiqua and Barbuda," *Countries of the World,* January 1, 1991.

Jonathan B. Tourtellot, "Unspoiled in Spite of Itself," *National Geographic Traveler*, November/December 2002.

Thomas E. Weil, "Haiti," *Countries of the World*, January 1, 1991.

Thomas E. Weil, Jan Knippers Black, Harold I. Blutstein, Kathyrn T. Johnson, Davis S. McNorris, and Frederick P. Munson, "Dominican Republic," *Countries of the World*, January 1, 1991.

Radio

Robert Siegel and Sally Watt, "Taino Indians," *All Things Considered*, National Public Radio, October 12, 1998.

Internet Sources

Amerindian Trail, "Carib Community Plans Amerindian Village," August 13, 2002. www.amerindiantrail.com.

———, "An Indian Rebellion in Trinidad, 1699," August 13, 2002. www.amerindiantrail.com.

———, "The Neglected Amerindian Heritage of TT," August 13, 2002. www.amerindiantrail.com.

Ivonne Figueroa, "Cultural History," *El Boricua—Taino of Puerto Rico,* August 13, 2002. www.elboricua.com.

Loida Figueroa, "History of Puerto Rico," *History of Puerto Rico—The Tainos Issue*, August 13, 2002. www.taino-tribe.org.

Government of the Jatibonicu Taino People, "A Letter to the Puerto Rican People," August 13, 2002. www.taino-tribe.org.

———, "Taino Culture," August 13, 2002. www.taino-tribe.org.

Anesa Hosien, "Caribs," *The Great Anesa,* August 13, 2002. http:// members.tripod.com.

Indigenous Dominica—The Caribs, "Caribs Yesterday and Today," August 13, 2002. www.geocities.com.

Indigenous People—The Caribs in Dominica, "The Carib Indians," August 13, 2002. www.avirtualdominica.com.

Jamaican History, "Columbus to the Destruction of Port Royal," August 13, 2002. www.discoverjamaica.com.

Kim Johnson, "The Taino," *Race and History*, August 13, 2002. www.raceandhistory.com

Margaret Morris, "The Land and the People," *Discover Jamaica*, August 13, 2002. www.discoverjamaica.com.

El Museo, "The Taino World," August 13, 2002. www.elmuseo.org.

Pre-Columbian Hispaniola, "Arawak-Taino Indians," August 13, 2002. www.hartford-hwp.com.

"Welcome to Trinidad and Tobago," *Santa Rosa Amerindian Community*, August 13, 2002, www.amerindiantrail.com.

———, "We the Carib Community of Trinidad and Tobago," August 13, 2002. http://members.tripod.com.

Richard L. Vasquez, "The Taino Survival," *Las Culturas*, August 13, 2002. www.lasculturas.com.

Websites

The Jatibonicu Taino Tribal National of Boriken (www.taino-tribe.org).

The United Confederation of Taino People (www.uctp.org).

Index

Picture Credits

Cover photo: © Peter Turnley/CORBIS
© Paul Almasy/CORBIS, 38
© Tom Bean/CORBIS, 29
© Bettmann/CORBIS, 62
© CORBIS, 27, 37, 40, 58
© Corel, 14, 18, 78, 82
Dover Publications, 44
© Karl Grobl, 68, 73, 74, 76
© Hulton/Archive by Getty Images, 8, 26
© Hulton-Deutsch Collection/CORBIS, 47
Chris Jouan, 7, 12, 45, 61
© Earl & Nazima Kowall/CORBIS, 71
© Bob Krist/CORBIS, 19, 63
Library of Congress, 11, 43, 48
© Maps.com/CORBIS, 46
North Wind Picture Archives, 55
© Neil Rabinowitz/CORBIS, 9
© Reuters NewMedia Inc./CORBIS, 23
© Manu Sassoonian/Art Resource, NY, 56
© Leonard de Selva/CORBIS, 34
© Snark/Art Resource, NY, 49, 65
© James A. Sugar/CORBIS, 30, 81

About the Author

Anne Wallace Sharp is the author of one adult book, *Gifts,* a compilation of stories about hospice patients, as well as several children's books, including *Daring Women Pirates* and five other books for Lucent Books. In addition, she has written numerous magazine articles for both the adult and children's market. A retired registered nurse, Sharp has a degree in history and a strong interest in indigenous people. Her other interests include reading, traveling, and spending time with her two grandchildren, Jacob and Nicole. Sharp lives in Beavercreek, Ohio.